EMPIRE OF LIBERTY

RE-MAPPING THE TRANSNATIONAL
A Dartmouth Series in American Studies

SERIES EDITOR
Donald E. Pease
Avalon Foundation Chair of Humanities
Founding Director of the Futures of American Studies Institute
Dartmouth College

The emergence of Transnational American Studies in the wake of the Cold War marks the most significant reconfiguration of American Studies since its inception. The shock waves generated by a newly globalized world order demanded an understanding of America's embeddedness within global and local processes rather than scholarly reaffirmations of its splendid isolation. The series Re-Mapping the Transnational seeks to foster the cross-national dialogues needed to sustain the vitality of this emergent field. To advance a truly comparativist understanding of this scholarly endeavor, Dartmouth College Press welcomes monographs from scholars both inside and outside the United States.

For a complete list of books available in this series, see www.upne.com.

Anthony Bogues, *Empire of Liberty: Power, Desire, and Freedom*

Bernd Herzogenrath, *An American Body\Politic: A Deleuzian Approach*

Johannes Voelz, *Transcendental Resistance: The New Americanists and Emerson's Challenge*

ANTHONY BOGUES

EMPIRE OF LIBERTY

Power, Desire, and Freedom

DARTMOUTH COLLEGE PRESS

HANOVER, NEW HAMPSHIRE

Published by
University Press of New England
Hanover and London

Dartmouth College Press
Published by University Press of New England
One Court Street, Lebanon NH 03766
www.upne.com
© 2010 Trustees of Dartmouth College
All rights reserved
Manufactured in the United States of America
Designed by Katherine B. Kimball
Typeset in Sabon by Integrated Publishing Solutions

University Press of New England is a member of the Green Press Initiative. The
paper used in this book meets their minimum requirement for recycled paper.

For permission to reproduce any of the material in this book, contact Permissions,
University Press of New England, One Court Street, Lebanon NH 03766; or visit
www.upne.com

Library of Congress Cataloging-in-Publication Data
Bogues, Anthony.
Empire of liberty : power, desire, and freedom / Anthony Bogues.
p. cm.—(Re-mapping the transnational)
Includes bibliographical references and index.
ISBN 978-1-58465-930-3 (cloth : alk. paper)—ISBN 978-1-58465-931-0 (pbk. : alk.
paper)
1. Liberty. 2. United States—Foreign relations—Philosophy. 3. United States—
Foreign relations—Moral and ethical aspects. 4. Imperialism—Moral and ethical
aspects. 5. Imperialism—Social aspects. I. Title.
JC585.B578 2010
327.73001—dc22   2010021296

5 4 3 2 1

To my grandmother Imogene
for all that she has taught me and
for my granddaughter Malia
with hopes for a more humane world.

CONTENTS

Acknowledgments ix

INTRODUCTION 1

1 EMPIRE OF LIBERTY
Desire, Power, and the States of Exception 9

2 RACE, HISTORICAL TRAUMA, AND DEMOCRACY
The Politics of a Historical Wrong 38

3 DEATH, POWER, VIOLENCE, AND NEW SOVEREIGNTIES 66

4 THE END OF HISTORY OR THE INVENTION OF EXISTENCE
Critical Thought and Thinking about the Human 98

Notes 123
Bibliography 141
Index 149

ACKNOWLEDGMENTS

BOTH THIS BOOK of essays and a platform to think and reflect aloud would not have been possible without the enormous generosity of Donald Pease. For a number of years we have been in dialogue about America. We have not agreed all the time, but Don's extraordinary insights always stimulate me to think again, even when I return to my original positions. Additionally, Don's broad and deep generosity, securely anchored in a rich conception of the life of the mind, has been a model in an academy driven by the marketization and banal professionalization of scholarship. Thank you, Don. Many ideas in these essays gestated in conversations with colleagues in the *boundary* 2 collective, particularly Ronald Judy, Paul Bové, Joe Buttigieg, and Hortense Spillers. Each of these colleagues has argued, agreed, or made objections known in different forums. For this I want to thank them. The other members of the *boundary* 2 collective have been an important intellectual source of criticism and support as I have stumbled through my efforts to understand America. The undergraduate students in my senior seminar class "Race, Empire, and Modernity," in the Africana Studies Department at Brown University, have quizzed, pushed back, and opened new lines of inquiry. I thank all the students who have taken this seminar. Brown University is a special place for undergraduate education, and the participation of these students in the seminar added immensely to the lectures and subsequent essays. When the lectures were revised, I had a series of conversations with the novelist John Edgar Wideman, who teaches at Brown. Those conversations found their way into the final revisions. Every lecturer needs an audience, and I could not have found a better one than those brave souls who came to hear all four of these lectures in the spring of 2007. Their questions and comments pushed me to reformulate many of my ideas, lecture after lecture, so that the four lectures became a single conversation with the audience over the course of time. It was a most stimulating intellectual experience, and my warmest thanks go to all those who attended these four talks. I also express much appreciation to Geri Augusto, who commented critically on some of the ideas in this book. Thanks as well to Dawn Jackson, who, when the manuscript was finally revised, did the work necessary to make sure that it arrived at the publisher on time. I want to thank Richard Pult and Amanda Dupuis of UPNE for the care and professionalism with which they managed the production of this book. Appreciation also to David Chu for fine copyediting.

The person who inspired me to think afresh and to ask questions anew was my grandmother Imogene Tulloch. As a child I had spent a great deal of time with her in rural Jamaica. Born two generations after slavery, she taught me with unmatched love, generosity, and sensitivity that there was nothing more important in the world than freedom and that, if one understood this, the world would be a better place. Her influence remains at the core of my life in many ways. I cannot repay my debt to her for the lessons she taught with love and care. In the end, I am responsible for the final content of this book, but I dedicate it to her. This book is also dedicated to my granddaughter Malia, who was born as I completed the final revisions to these lectures.

Anthony Bogues
Providence
August 2009

INTRODUCTION

THE LECTURES COLLECTED here were delivered at Dartmouth College in the spring of 2007 to inaugurate the Freedman Humanities Lecture Series. With the exception of the second essay, "Race, Historical Trauma, and Democracy: The Politics of a Historical Wrong," the essays have been edited only to reflect the different format in which they are now presented. It has been a delicate balancing act, keeping to the narrative style of a lecture or conversation while editing so that a reader may follow the arguments. The second essay reflects material from a lecture titled "W. E. B. DuBois, *Black Reconstruction,* Slave Emancipation, and American Democracy," delivered at Dartmouth College for the Futures of American Studies Institute in June 2008. So in a deep sense all the essays and ideas presented here were made possible by the creative intellectual space which Dartmouth College has afforded me over the past few years, first as a visiting humanities scholar and then as a regular summer faculty member of the Futures of American Studies Institute.

My theme for the Freedman Humanities Lecture Series was "Empire of Liberty: Power, Desire, and Freedom." I chose this theme because, for the past five years or so, I have been thinking about what it means to live *inside* an empire. Living in Jamaica for many years, I was preoccupied with the nature of imperial power and the external drives of that power as it impacted the Caribbean and Africa, particularly its military interventions and its none-too-subtle economic coercions through multilateral institutions such as the International Monetary Fund (IMF) and the World Bank. My political experiences made me aware of the capacity of an imperial power to wield undue political influence through either overt or covert means. Living in the Caribbean, I came of age in the early aftermath of Jamaica's political independence. Thus I was very aware of the operations of colonial power. In Jamaica, constitutional decolonization had created a juridically independent nation-state, but hundreds of years of colonial domination had left stubborn structural legacies. Of those many legacies one of the most powerful was the effort by colonial power to reform the so-called native mind. I considered this feature of colonial power to be the ideological weight of colonial domination. I always felt it was a critical feature because it illuminated an aspect of power which, in the heat of radical political activity, we did not pay sufficient attention to. It was not just a matter of the ways in which dominant ideas worked by setting limits or establishing horizons that were then taken for granted. Instead, those ideas were inhabited and then came to map our social world. Years ago, Louis Althusser argued that the materiality of ideology produced subjects in what Stuart Hall, invoking Ernesto Laclau, described as a "chain of linked interpellations that constitute the Imaginary."[1] If one of our human labors was or is always upon ourselves, then it seemed to me that power always has to find ways in which it can capture that labor. Over time, but particularly when I moved to the United States, it became clear to me that my initial preoccupations with questions of ideology were insufficient for grappling with the present constitution of power. This insufficiency became acute as I listened carefully to discussions and debates about the Iraq war and the responses to the tragedy of 9/11. It was at this point that I began a study of American political thought as I had never done before.

In this enterprise I discovered that the most perceptive writer and scholar on American society was W. E. B. DuBois. Whether it was *The Souls of Black Folk*, *Black Reconstruction*, the hundreds of essays he wrote, or the many books he published, DuBois's life and work represented a most remarkable attempt both to understand America and to change it. It was only then that I came to fully understand C. L. R. James's assessment of DuBois, which I had read some twenty years before. James remarks of DuBois, "There is no need to subscribe to all that Dr Du Bois has said and done. But long before the rulers and the leaders of thought in the United States grasped the essentials of the world in which they lived Dr Du Bois did, and to look upon him just as a great leader of the Negro people or just a true son of Africa is to diminish the conceptions and mitigate the impact of one of the greatest citizens of the modern world."[2] There was another reason why DuBois appealed to me. Not only was he a person of both word and deed and was a scholar with what we call today deep activist commitments, but DuBois moved seamlessly across many disciplinary fields. In this effort what drove him was seeking answers to questions that troubled him. But it was not a self-interested effort, it was one guided by a commitment to changing the world. It became clear to me as I reread and listened afresh to DuBois as well as many of the novelists, thinkers, musicians, artists, and writers of what can be called the radical black intellectual tradition that what had made that tradition distinctive were the questions it had posed.

In 2002 I began to write a series of essays exploring this tradition.[3] By the time I was asked to deliver the Freedman lectures, I was in a position to speak and think *with* and *through* this tradition while taking into account other questions posed by thinkers not operating within the tradition. I owe the reader this brief intellectual history because it situates these lectures and the concerns that drove them.

In the late 1970s and '80s the political axis of the West shifted with the electoral victories of Ronald Reagan, Margaret Thatcher, and

Helmut Kohl. The emergence of these three figures at the same moment signaled a decisive shift in electoral political terms and in ideological framing ones. These political figures set out to change the terms of contemporary political discourse and for a time successfully defined those terms. At the heart of this change was the elevation of the market into an ethic. As an ethic the market became, in Antonio Gramsci's phrase, "common sense." Ronald Judy reminds us that common sense is the "designation for that agency which organizes and enables intentional purposive human activity."[4] However, for this common sense to consolidate itself, a language had to be found that could stabilize the primacy of the market ethic for at least some time. The organizing language for this new ethic was a conception of "freedom." Thus, as neoliberalism became the dominant ideology of imperial power, it worked through an ideological space in which "freedom" became the "common sense." It was a remarkable deployment of a term invested with a particular conception of freedom, which could conjure up the deepest feelings that organize our lives.

My sojourn in America coincided with the Bush regime's biopolitical settlement and an attempt to institute a profoundly neoconservative project.[5] Under the rubric of "the American Century," this project called for America to exercise benevolent global hegemony. It advocated a mixture of positions requiring America to control the international commons of cyberspace and the development of global missile defense systems that could secure American power around the world. These lectures were delivered against the backdrop of the falling apart of this project as the consequences of the Iraq war created fissures amongst the leading figures in the project. These fissures could also be seen within significant segments of the American population, who began to question the legitimacy of the war.

In these lectures I attempt in broad strokes to understand this neoconservative project not as an aberration of American civilization but as one of its many logics. These logics are rooted in a historical trajectory of dominant practices in America's political history. The lectures therefore are not concerned with the cut and thrust of the Bush bio-political settlement and its unraveling but rather seek to understand a different logic which may have been operating. My goal has been to think about the character of American hegemony and to ask: what does it presently illuminate about power? As I grappled with this question it became clear to me that American power, while functioning in the conventional ways of all imperial powers (for instance, through military interventions, economic domination, and civilizing missions), had a unique quality about it. This was not strange. All imperial powers have unique features. America was an empire, but what kind of empire was it? During the Bush regime many pages were written on the subject. However, it was Thomas Jefferson's phrase "empire of liberty," appropriated from Edmund Burke, which gave me insight into what I consider to be a special feature of American imperial power.

Jefferson began to use the phrase "empire of liberty" while arguing for the expansion of the Union. Merrill Peterson has suggested that for Jefferson, "Liberty was the ultimate value, the Union the means to be cherished only so long as it furthered the end of its being."[6] Thus, it seems to me a couple of things are clear. First, at the moment when "freedom" was being constructed as "common sense," it was not a rhetorical cover for imperial adventure, but rather imperial power was developing a technology of rule that had been deployed during previous colonial empires. It was a technology of rule in which the creation of new subjectivities was paramount. Second, this configuration of power was occurring in a global context in which radical ideas and movements had generally declined. I therefore felt that Jefferson's "empire of liberty" was not a metaphor for something else but was a description of a project of power in which the possibility of total domination was the horizon.

The four lectures presented here center on a set of questions and issues about "empire of liberty" and its significance as a project of power: the issues of race and history, the questions of violence, and, finally, critical thought today. In all of the lectures, there are some words that serve as keywords, bringing together ideas and arguments into a network of reflections upon the time we presently inhabit. Of course, the questions of how power can be resisted today and of what possibilities exist for a different kind of freedom than imperial freedom haunt these lectures. In thinking about these questions, I found it useful to return to the theories and practices of radical anticolonial thinking as one possible basis from which to develop critical thought. Not that all other currents of radical thought are exhausted, but important insights may be gleaned from radical critiques that begin their analysis from the ground on which the native or racialized body had to construct the human with new meanings.

The first lecture, titled "Empire of Liberty: Desire, Power, and the States of Exception," sets the stage and establishes the grounds for some of the arguments in the rest of the lectures. Not only does it discuss the meanings and operations of this "empire of liberty," but it argues that, if at one time power worked through ideology as interpellation to create subjects, today power strives to capture desire and imagination. This lecture is followed by "Race, Historical Trauma, and Democracy: The Politics of a Historical Wrong," in which I think about democracy not as an absence or a formal theory of rights but rather as an intense and intimate experience within a polity. In this lecture I complicate Aristotle's notion of the *zoon politikon* by arguing that human beings are not made for life in the polis in some innate way but rather must struggle to construct and invent *ways of life* that allow us to practice forms of democracy. I argue that our concern with ways of life enables us to make democracy. In this lecture I also suggest that the voyages of Vasco da Gama and Christopher Columbus inaugurated an epoch of human history in which both colonialism and racial slavery profoundly shaped our ways of life for many centuries. Both these voyages shattered St. Augustine's conception of the fabled antipodes where human beings lived hanging upside down. While overturning this Western conception, the voyages opened the way for the institution of a hierarchical system of classification of human beings. In this system, difference and discontinuity in the gaze of the Western observer became linked to conceptions of historical progress, and race became a determining factor for human status. Therefore we should not think about questions of democracy without acknowledging DuBois's epigraph to the first chapter of *Black Reconstruction*: "How Black men coming to America in the 16th and 17th centuries became a central thread in the history of the United States and at once a challenge to its democracy."[7] The second lecture does not argue that race and colonial power created the conditions for democracy to be an unfinished project, an argument which assumes that democracy is really constructed around issues of inclusion and exclusion. Rather it suggests that if democracy requires intimacy then it has to reckon with the sustained legacies of historical injustice and historical trauma. In the end I argue that democracy is not really about procedures but, as Jacques Rancière notes, is embodied "in the very forms of concrete life and sensible experience."[8] The third essay, titled "Death, Power, Violence, and New Sovereignties," attempts to think about death as a form of politics. Death has become a haunting specter in the contemporary world. In this essay, I reflect on genocide and violence in general. I also review the character of violence in the postcolony. Reflecting on both genocide and violence, I argue that death and violence are linked to performances of power as a further illustration that power itself is performative. As power seeks to become a totality, it desires to *command life itself.* In this form of domination, the bio-political moment is not one, in Michel Foucault's phrase, of "make live" or "let die," nor is it about the exercise of power as the right of the sword. Instead, it is about creating conditions of life where death is acceptable. In such a context, violence does not evacuate power—it is power.

The final lecture asks the perennial question, an ethical, intellectual, and political one. What resources do we have today that may allow us to think our way out of the various conundrums that we currently face? Working through the title "The End of History or the Invention of Existence: Critical Thought and Thinking about the Human," this lecture takes up the question of humanism in critical thought from the perspective of a twentieth-century, radical, anti-colonial tradition. Arguing that conventional critical theory has been epistemically blind, I invoke the writings of Frantz Fanon as a starting point to begin thinking differently about the world today. I argue that there is a politics of imagination that is central to any contemporary project of human freedom. So while the essays begin with Thomas Jefferson's phrase "empire of liberty" in an exploration of the nature of American imperial power as empire, they end with a discussion of freedom. It is freedom seen from the perspective of those who were unfree, from what the Latin American intellectual Enrique Dussell calls the "underside of modernity." In the end, the concerns in these lectures center on the human practices of thinking about and trying to live ways of life that are constructed around forms of freedom that are about human creativity instead of domination. If the essays provoke discussion and reflection by the reader about what these freedom practices might look like, then their publication has been worthwhile.

[1]

EMPIRE OF LIBERTY

Desire, Power, and the States
of Exception

And we Americans are the peculiar, chosen people—the Israel of
Our time; we bear the ark of the liberties of the world . . .
God has predestined. Mankind expects, great things from our race
. . . indeed the political messiah has come. But he has come in us.

—HERMAN MELVILLE

The empire and the garden. We are to speak of them the same way. They belong to the
same person. They both belong to God.   —GEORGE LAMMING

We go on creating what mankind calls an empire while we continue to believe quite
sincerely that it is not an empire because it does not feel to us the way we imagine an
empire ought to feel.   —WALTER LIPPMANN

OVER THE PAST few years there has been a vigorous debate about
the character of America as an imperial power and empire.[1] The
parameters of this debate center on questions about the kind of
imperial power that the current configuration of American power
represents. Does American imperial power follow the models of
European colonial empires? Or is American imperial power primarily military, engaging in actions of an unprecedented character in an
age of asymmetrical warfare? Or is American power the only super-
power in a unipolar world? Central to this debate are definitional
issues. For example, does American power meet the definitional re-
quirements of empire?[2] Of course, in addition to these questions,

there is the perennial one in American political thought: can a republic be an imperial power? Are the political logics of a republic commensurate with empire?[3] I wish to begin probing these issues by recalling three earlier meanings of empire. I begin with a reminder that the Latin root of empire is *imperium*, meaning rule and command. It is an important reminder, since in much of the current definitional debate about empire, rule and command, and therefore a certain conception of power, tend to be neglected. Instead, the debate about empire focuses on issues of territorial acquisition, military strength, and force. On the other hand, some thinkers, including Michael Hardt and Antonio Negri, have argued that empire now means a "logic and structure of rule."[4] For them this structure and form is about a "new notion of right, or rather, a new inscription of authority."[5] Although one never clearly grasps the precise nature of this new right, the authors accurately point us to thinking about the novel ways in which power operates today. One definition of empire that has become popular is given by the historian Dominic Lieven. He notes that empire is:

> First and foremost a very great power that has left its mark on the international relations of the era . . . a polity that rules over wide territories and many peoples . . . an empire is by definition not a polity [that] rules with the explicit consent of its peoples.[6]

This definition has been accepted by commentators and scholars in various attempts to slot modern American power into a definitional box. This search for a conventional definition, while useful, may play tricks with one's thinking. For instance, what happens when the form of imperial rule does not require territories as we have come to understand them, when power constructs rule primarily through self-regulation? Does that make power imperial or not?

My second observation about empire draws upon Pierre Manent's comment that the central political problem in European political history after the dissolution of the Roman Empire was "what were the political forms at men's disposal after this event?"[7] Observing that the Holy Roman Empire officially ended in 1806, Manent suggests that the consistent content of the idea of empire was "the bringing together of all the known world, of the *orbis terrarum*, under a unique power. . . . It corresponds instead to men's unity, to the universality of human nature, which wants to be recognized and addressed by a unique power."[8] This conception of a "unique power" and its universal dispositions commensurate with human nature has been at the core of all major imperial powers.[9] As such, some critical questions we face are: What are the languages and practices of empire today? And how does empire represent its unique power?

The third meaning of empire I wish to recall is closely allied to the first, but it is a more precise definition of "unique power." The Roman philosopher and statesman Cicero noted that, while Roman roads and architecture were integral to the success of the Roman Empire, *pax Romana* was constructed on *ways of living* that were based on "our wise grasp of a single truth."[10] This "single truth" was embodied in the phrase *civis Romanus sum* (I am a Roman citizen). The imperial political formulation of *civis Romanus sum* was, in Cicero's phrase, "a single joint community of gods and men."[11] Here we come to an aspect of empire not often examined. Cicero's phrase should give us pause. It suggests that imperial power is also about establishing ways of life that rest on a single truth determined by power as common to human nature. Cicero's conception of empire has been central to different forms of imperial power that typically operate under the language of "civilizing missions." In this regard American imperial power, with its practices of representative democracy and free markets, which are then deployed as "freedom," is no different. However, there are differences between various forms of imperial power. American power, while based on military power and violence, draws extensively from two other things. The first is a notion of representative democracy and liberal freedom as the single truth that must be grasped by all humanity. Second, at the level of language, American imperial power takes seriously the deployment of a form of power by which self-regulated, individual subjectivity meshes with the drives of the imperium.[12] At this point I am not referring simply to ideological hegemony. Rather, I am pointing to ways in which American imperial power in its present configuration seeks to capture desire and imagination, to consolidate its single truth as the *only* way of life, thereby confirming to itself and us that we are indeed at the end of history. Winston Churchill, whose political career coincided with the demise of the British colonial empire, remarked at a lecture at Harvard University in 1943, a few years before the political independence of India, that "the empires of the future are the empires of the mind."[13] It was a telling comment because, reflecting on the demise of Britain's colonial empire, Churchill saw clearly that the political sustainability of empire as a form of rule was only possible with the self-regulation of subjectivity through processes of interpellation.

To tell a story of America as an imperial power, of its desire for a unique kind of domination, requires us not only to tell a different narrative of American power but to think about the question: What are we as humans? It also requires us to ask the question: how shall we live together? Michel Foucault notes that when Kant asked the question, "What is the Enlightenment?" he really was asking: What is happening at a specific historical moment? In the twentieth century, perhaps four issues have shaped our long-term political understandings: colonial power, various forms of racial domination, fascism, and liberalism in its various guises. Three of the four have been historical hinges, that is, they have been events in which we have had to ask ourselves: what kind of life is possible after colonial domination, racial domination, and fascism? What I am suggesting is that our contemporary moment is one such historical hinge, at which the question about what is happening to us is a global one. This is the importance of grappling with the "empire of liberty" as a modality of power today. I now wish to place a caveat on the table before we proceed. I do not intend to present an entire theory, nor do I wish to engage in formal theory-building in these lectures.

Rather I hope to point to a set of directions that may facilitate an understanding of the present. So with that let us move on to the "empire of liberty."

Empire of Liberty

How might one think about empire today? I have already indicated that my focus will be on ways of life, about how power constructs subjectivities. As a precursor to this, I turn to a set of historical discourses and material practices that shaped the emergence of the American "empire of liberty."

In American intellectual and political history, liberty quickly came to mean self-government. In 1776 Richard Price noted that liberty rested upon "the idea of self-direction or self-government."[14] In this regard Lockean ideas of natural liberty and the civic republicanism of this period operated on similar grounds, even though they emerged out of two distinct intellectual traditions. To have an imperium based on notions of self-government at first seemed improbable. However, the answer to this apparent difficulty resides in our capacity to think about the precise practices of liberty as self-government and to find the language that will allow for that understanding.

For this purpose, Thomas Jefferson's phrase "empire of liberty" is apt. Writing about the nature of America's westward ambition, Jefferson redeployed Edmund Burke's phrase and attributed to American power the historic role of creating an empire of liberty. At the level of political language, this designation signaled certain forms of power. While conventional imperial rule usually meant violence that originated in founding violence, for Jefferson an empire of liberty was possible because a state could "conquer without war." In a letter to Thomas Pinckney, Jefferson noted that war was "not the best engine for us to resort to."[15] Thus, at the level of political language and affect, an empire of liberty conjured up a different project of imperial power than the conventional colonial one. Julian

Boyd describes Jefferson's conception of an empire of liberty in some detail:

> Though he called [it] an Empire of Liberty . . . it was to be neither an isolated political entity nor an imperialistic force for compulsory extension of ideals of liberty. Its domain and compulsions would be in the realm of the mind and spirit of man . . . incapable of being restrained, and holding imperial sway not by arms or political power but by the sheer majesty of ideas and ideals.[16]

Thus for Jefferson force was still necessary for rule within the empire of liberty, but the sustainability of its political power resided in the realm of the mind and in bending consciousness to conform to what was seen as the natural spirit of being human. An empire of liberty as imperial power therefore recognized the natural unfolding of human destiny as embodied in ways of life that were founded on conceptions of American liberty. At the level of political discourse, coercive force is perceived to be absent from this unfolding, and, when perchance force is deployed, it is with regret. However, this is a paradox, because conquest is a consequence of war. Jefferson's empire of liberty implied that American power needed to wage a different kind of war, not military battles but wars in which humankind would come to recognize that America was "the sole depository of the sacred fire of freedom and self-government, from hence it is to be lighted up in other regions of the earth."[17] This was a war to construct ways of life. In this regard the American empire of liberty distinguishes itself from imperial Rome, where citizenship was seen as the essential ingredient of *pax Romana*. Instead, *pax Americana* requires acceptance of the single truth expressed most aptly during the period of neoconservatism by Roger Kaplan:

> the purpose of power is not power itself; it is a fundamentally liberal purpose of sustaining the key characteristics of an orderly world. Those characteristics include basic political stability, the idea of liberty . . . respect for property, economic freedom and representative government.[18]

Critical to such a project is the representation of America. We are aware today that the modern can be staged as representation. I would argue that, depending on the force of the representation and its embeddings in a set of historical events, representation has a capacity to incorporate a self-narrative, which creates a material life that enters into the social architecture of the lived experience of the world, thereby creating a distinctive imagination of the real. Central to this is language. When the discourse of a specific representation becomes all-powerful, we do not become bewitched by the language games of grammar, but rather a word, a discourse, takes on a life in which we invest desire. Raymond Williams has suggested that some words are "strong words." Such words have conceptual values; they invoke and define. I suggest that liberty is one such word and that when it becomes the single organizing truth it provides the ground for one series of political practices.

Historically, America's westward push was conducted at the expense of the Native American population. In the nineteenth century, this push involved a war with Mexico and the military defeat of many Native American groups. The symbolic code that organized this push was embodied in the phrase "manifest destiny," the idea that America's expansion was part of its providential design. This design was at the core of the formation of the American Republic. At the inauguration of the republic, even the most radical of thinkers believed in this design. Thomas Paine, for example, invested the new republic with the power to create an entire new world when he remarked in 1776, "We have it in our power to begin the world all over again."[19] Others like Joel Barlow compared the birth of the republic to that of a savior of global proportions. This idea of America as the force for regeneration of the world was expressed at the beginning of the twentieth century by Albert Beveridge who remarked that "God had made us the master organizers of the world. He has marked the American people as his chosen nation to finally lead in the regeneration of the world. This is the divine mission of America."[20] There has been since its inauguration the idea of American power as the ultimate power on the planet. One of my arguments is that the discourse that has surrounded this power has been constructed around the idea of liberty.

One may summarize the emergence and consolidation of America as an imperial power in three phases. In the first, there is the process of internal territorial conquest of Native American land and the social and political defeat of this population. In the second, there is an external push through which a few territories are acquired. In this second phase, there are also numerous interventions in Latin America and the Caribbean, primarily focused on bolstering American economic strength.[21] In these two phases the system of racial slavery and racial domination are of course central elements. In the third and current phase, while economics is important (as it is quite frankly central in all phases), the key objectives are attempts of American power to create ways of life.

The historian William Appleman Williams has already argued for this conception of American empire.[22] However, his deployment of the phrase _ways of life_ speaks mostly to historical continuities within American history. I want to use this phrase with a different tone and meaning. Ways of life are forms of human living, they are thoughts and practices that define and create our human world as well as modes of belonging to a society. Hannah Arendt once observed that the singular fact that creates politics is that ". . . men, not Man, live on the earth and inhabit the world."[23] From this stance, Michel Foucault poses a critical question: how are human beings made subjects? This question, I wish to suggest, is the central political question of our time. Thus the contemporary political problem is not about how we are ruled, about sovereignty in the conventional sense of thinking about political obligation. Instead I pose other questions: What kind of human beings are we? And how therefore shall we live? This is a difficult point to grasp for two reasons. The first is that, for many places around the world, "necropolitics" is the order of the day, making death and violence everyday political norms. Very often in our response to this, we turn our eyes away from the spectacle of violence and seek refuge in forms of liberalism. When we do this, we transpose our preoccupation with order into a preoccupation with security, and fear drives our short-term political sentiments. Second, at the sites where liberalism has split the public and the private, the dominant argument is that there are no major political problems that cannot be solved by contemporary mechanisms of rule. In both these instances, the political is nested within questions of how we are ruled, and as a consequence we study the various technologies of power centering on forms of what is called democracy. My argument is simply that this question of rule is no longer structured around questions of political obligation but rather around creating subjectivities.

The question of rule, who should rule and how it should be done, as well as issues of legitimacy, were the historic, central questions for the nation-state. In the contemporary period, these questions are not unimportant, because, as Foucault reminds us, a new technology of power does not exclude the former one but "modif[ies] it to some extent . . . makes use of very different instruments."[24] However, if one feature of our modernity in its colonial incarnation was how to conquer and control bodies (slaves and natives), then today the political field is global, and, in addition to conquest by force, there is an emphasis on the creation of political and social subjectivities. This does not negate the drive for violence, but it does point to an important dialectic between coercion and hegemony and to power's rearrangement of its modalities of domination.

Today liberal power (a dominant form of power) has shifted its focus and seeks to move beyond its historic bio-political moment. To put this another way, if Foucault is right that biopolitics deals with the population "as a problem that is at once scientific and political . . . as a biological problem and as power's problem" and that the nub of governmentality is now directed to "man-as-species," then, I would argue, the drive for power, while still directed at "man-as-species," wishes to regularize power through the construction of ways of life and modes of self-regulation.[25] To my mind this makes

the moment a *bios-political* one, that is, one in which both subjectivities and the imagination carry tremendous weight in the operations of power. Thus I would argue that one critical element of the
repertoire of power today is <u>a drive to capture desire</u>. There are two
genealogical tracks that I will now follow to illustrate this point. The
first one tracks power in the conventional way, in the emergence of
liberal power through sovereignty. The second track follows the
emergence of power through coloniality. These are analytically distinct, but I want to draw out a set of relationships between them.

The Tracking of Power

As discussed earlier, when sovereignty emerges in Western thought,
it concerns itself with the questions of political obligation and rule.
Issues having to do with nationality and territory are attached to
the emergence of sovereignty. One account of the emergence of sovereignty claims that rights operate in a double way. First, there are
natural rights, and second, some of these rights are given up so that
governance can occur. There is disagreement, as we know, in the
case of Hobbes. For Hobbes, sovereign power is about security, for
Locke and others, it is about creating the context for the mainte-
nance of natural rights. This is more or less the conventional story in
political theory about the emergence of sovereign power and natural rights theory. However, Foucault leaves that story behind. In a
remarkable essay titled "Subject and Power," he provides a genealogy of power in which he pays attention to what he calls the "tricky
combination in the same political structures of individualization
techniques and of totalization procedures."[26] Foucault identifies
the origins of this form of power in Christian institutions and calls
it "pastoral power." He tells us that pastoral power is a form of
power "whose ultimate aim is to assure individual salvation in the
next world."[27]

For Foucault, and in accordance with the argument that I am
making, the most important feature of pastoral power was its con-

figuration as a form of power which could not be exercised "without knowing the inside of people's minds, without exploring their souls, without making them reveal their innermost secrets. It implies a knowledge of the conscience and an ability to direct it."[28] This ecclesiastical mode of power spread beyond its original location and in time became a major feature of power. In this shift, knowledge of conscience was replaced by a drive to capture desire and reshape it. Two historic events made this possible.

The first event was the abolition of racial slavery in the Atlantic world and the subsequent debates in both colonial British and American circles about what the ex-slave should become. (I will return to these debates later.) The second event occurred with the economic and accompanying discursive transformations in America in the late nineteenth and early twentieth centuries. Regarding the latter, William Leach makes the point that, by the 1880s, attempts were made to transform the dominant discourse about American society from "land of comfort" to "land of desire."[29] He further argues that by 1912 American culture had become preoccupied with "consumption as a means to reach happiness, the cult of the new, the democratization of desire."[30] This is an important plank of my argument. A review of the debates about how to produce consumer consciousness in the late nineteenth and twentieth centuries reveals a great deal. With the emergence of mass production, the dominant social classes needed to tap into the imagination of other sections of the American populace. In an article on advertising published in 1901, Fogg Mead noted that the successful creation of a mass consumer required creating within an individual the "ability to want and choose" and therefore "opening up imagination and emotion to desire."[31] Leach points us to Katherine Fisher, another advertising expert, who in 1899 wrote "*Without imagination, no wants*" (emphasis mine).[32] As American capitalism transformed itself in the twentieth century, the United States became a society in which the world of consumption was synonymous with the meaning of freedom. A form of rule that required the self-regulation of subjects accompanied this shift. It was at this point that the technologies of rule developed inside coloniality began to find resonance in the ways power now had to operate. So let us for a brief moment track this second incarnation of power, colonial power.

Sovereign colonial power, as Achille Mbembe makes clear, operates on command and violence. It converts its "foundational violence into an authorizing authority."[33] The defining feature of colonial sovereignty was "might is right," the right of the sword. But colonial sovereignty had other facets of rule. In constructing rule, it also had to make fundamental attempts to shape the consciousness of the so-called native. All the European colonial powers had this drive. However, I wish to use French colonial power as an example, because there are unusual parallels with some issues seen today, particularly those concerning the relationship between a republic and an empire. As Raymond Williams tells us in *Keywords*, when the word *civilization* was used in the eighteenth century, it was in opposition to barbarity.[34] In France, the colonial civilizing mission called *mission civilisatrice* rested upon, as Alice Conklin tells us, "the fundamental assumptions about the superiority of French Culture and the perfectibility of humankind."[35] By the late nineteenth century, French politicians were arguing that "We must believe that if Providence deigned to confer upon us a mission by making us masters of earth, this mission consists not of attempting an impossible fusion of the races but of simply spreading or awakening among other races, the superior notions of which we are the guardians."[36] The question that divided French politics at the time was not over the ethics of colonialism but over *how* to implement the best form of colonial power with its civilizing mission.

In other words, could there be conquest without war?[37] For liberal power, I would argue, whenever this dilemma about the possibility of conquest without war occurred, it was typically resolved in such a manner that war and the civilizing mission went hand in hand. Historically, therefore, this supposed dilemma has never stopped the forward march of colonial power and conquest. However, as stated earlier, there were other aspects to colonial power. Frantz Fanon made it clear that colonial power "reformed" the "native's mind." Writing in 1952's *Black Skin, White Masks*, Fanon notes that "To speak means to be in a position to use a certain syntax, to grasp the morphology of this or that language, but it means above all to assume a culture, to support the weight of a civilization."[38] To create the new subjectivities of the colonized, colonial power insisted on colonial language and used that language to transform desire and therefore imagination. What is the nub of my argument here? It is this: the technologies of colonial power were not only central to twentieth-century fascism, as Arendt, Césaire, and others have reminded us, but they continue to shape power's deployment. While ruling colonies with force, colonial power also had to manage subjectivities. I suggest that today this management of subjectivities has become a basic political requirement of liberal power.

If, during the period of colonial modernity, the political economy of exploitation was the central feature of the colonial project, alongside missions of civilization, then by the nineteenth century, liberalism moved to locate the civilizing mission and thereby subject formation and ways of life to the center of the colonial project. One of the most important events signaling this shift was the abolition of racial slavery in the Caribbean.[39] It is significant that many theorists concerned with a genealogy of liberal power, including Foucault, do not mention or examine this event. Yet one cannot read some of the writings of John Stuart Mill, one of the most important nineteenth-century liberal theorists, without thinking about the specters of slavery and the colonial project.[40] American imperial power, in its current phase and with all its complexities, allows us to examine how liberal power deepens this element of the construction of ways of life as central to the current repertoire of imperial power. The conditions for the performances of American imperial power in the contemporary geopolitical space are new today. One feature of this space since the end of the Cold War is the idea that, for the first time since the beginning of the twentieth century, a single truth can now be imposed upon all human populations. Listen to sections of President Bush's national security speech from 2003. The president proclaims that "the advance of freedom is the calling of our time; it is the calling of our country. . . . we believe that liberty is the design of nature; we believe that liberty is the direction of history."[41] Is it not clear that the drive of American imperial power is to trap human life within this framework of a single truth, of liberty, in order to achieve America's destiny? Some time ago, Sacvan Bercovitch noted how biblical history had been incorporated into American thought and experiences. Bercovitch observed that this incorporation "consecrated the American present as a movement from promise to fulfillment, and translated fulfillment from its meaning within the closed system of sacred history into a metaphor for limitless secular improvement."[42] Over time, American liberty has become the metaphor not only for human improvement but for the definitive way in which humankind is to construct ways of living.

In political terms, this American liberty, this unique, single truth, can be expressed within liberalism. Here I wish to move away from the common American party-political use of the term. Liberalism in different guises is America's governing political code and political language. As a political theory of modernity, liberalism posits tenets about the moral primacy of the individual within the foundations of a market economy. As John Gray notes, liberalism in its discourses on toleration requires that "liberal institutions are seen as applications of universal principles."[43] The revival of earlier conceptions of liberalism in the present period, sometimes in opposition to elements of liberalism that developed in the twentieth century, has not transformed liberal political theory into something else. Neoliberalism intersects with liberalism. There is a way in which the "tricky ground of liberalism as a *final* way of life creates the conditions for a conception of imperial power which calls itself 'imperial liberalism.'" Robert Cooper, a key advocate of this view, notes that:

We have chosen to do good rather than to be powerful. Torture is unacceptable not just because it is ineffective, but because our system is based on respect for individual people. Europeans talk of human rights and the rule of law while Americans talk of freedom and democracy, but they mean the same thing. For America, the way to be good in a world of power used to be to isolate itself. That is no longer possible. Instead it seeks to remake the world in its image. This is the European project also. . . . There are many ways we can assist short of employing force—using military power to provide security is one of them—but in the end it is the force of the idea and the power of its practice that conquers. Liberal imperialism may be an oxymoron, but *imperial liberalism* may be the reality of today[44] (emphasis mine).

This "imperial liberalism" can be understood as an "empire of liberty." So far I have characterized American imperial power as an empire of liberty, an empire in which conceptions of American liberty are the single truth. I wish to do two things now. First, I want to make a set of arguments about this empire of liberty as a phenomenon that goes beyond our common understanding of ideology. Second, I want to describe more precisely what the characteristics of this American liberty are.

Ideology and American Power

Louis Althusser tells us that there is a materiality to ideology, not only in its rituals but also in the effect of its practices. Although Althusser develops a rigid schema when discussing the relationship between the subject and ideology, he is correct to point out that "the category of the subject is only constitutive of all ideology insofar as all ideology has the function (which defines it) of 'constituting' concrete individuals as subjects."[45] For Althusser, ideology interpellates individuals as subjects. Stuart Hall and others have critiqued this notion of ideology and its place in reproductive articulations of society as too integrative and functionalist. I agree with this criticism but think that Althusser's point about St. Paul should be kept in mind. Althusser writes, "As St. Paul admirably put it, it is in the 'Logos,' meaning ideology, that we 'live, move and have our being.'"[46] How we "live, move and have our being" constitutes our ways of life. Following this approach, we could say that American liberty is a dominant ideology that has us in thralldom, and that what is needed in radical politics is a counterideology. And in one sense this is accurate. But we face a difficulty going down that path. What is the language of the counterideology when liberty is in many ways already captured? Can we deploy liberty or freedom as a general counterclaim? And if we do, then what might it mean? The real conundrum here is that liberty has become central to the signification system of liberalism and as a word performs political action. It is a speech-act that, in its language performances, is not a distortion, nor does it operate as a metaphoric trope. It has become a master key in the language of liberal political discourse. Thus we have to ask, what work does this word do? How does it shape subjectivity? Human subjectivity is of course one part of a large network of discursive formations and practices, but, before proceeding any further, I turn to one of the most important essays written by Raymond Williams, "The Analysis of Culture." Grappling with the problem of how to characterize culture neither as pattern nor as character but as part of an actual experience through which humans live and have experience, Williams argues that culture is really a "structure of feeling."[47] Since 1961, when Williams promulgated this idea, there has been much debate. However, in this lecture I want to think about how a word such as liberty can generate a "structure of feeling," not as an act of culture, but as a word that represents so much about ourselves and how we may wish to live, or at least presents the possibilities of how we might live, that the word itself takes on a life in which it becomes a feeling rooted in desire. It is in this sense that I wish to posit liberty, or freedom, as one node in the formation of subjectivity. Liberty as a word becomes a container, which we may fill with different things.

From the point of view of American power, President Bush recently described American liberty in the 2002 document *National Security Strategy of the United States*. The opening sentences of this document sum up the idea of a single truth, proclaiming "The great struggles of the twentieth century between liberty and totalitarianism ended with a decisive victory for the forces of freedom—*and a single sustainable model for national success: Freedom, democracy, and free enterprise.*"[48]

In the general geopolitical moment we inhabit, American power feels specifically that the global political field is open for the construction of its empire of liberty. In order to achieve this outcome, it is critical to implement power so as to capture desire and imagination. It is this exercise of a modality of power that seeks to go beyond ideology as we know it that I wish to draw your attention to. This is not simply a question of "soft power," as Joseph Nye and others have argued. This is about creating power of a certain type. If Lacan is correct that there is a diachronic aspect to everyday desire and that this desire can be articulated through demand,[49] then the next logical step in power's ability to create subjects would be to capture desire and in turn to create a certain kind of subject who is a particular human being. In this regard, I think Sylvia Wynter is correct in pointing us to the ways in which bourgeois society has created *homo oeconomicus*.[50]

This activity of power, which attempts to capture desire and imagination, has two dimensions that I want to point out. In the first, capitalism and market economics have created a way of life that Zygmunt Bauman has called "consuming life."[51] This way of life can be summed up in an advertising slogan I saw in a London department store in 2004. The sign read: *I shop therefore I am.*

In the second dimension, power in performing hegemony seeks to close all the possible gaps through which the imagination of alternatives is desired. In this drive, power attempts to shut out all possibly different futures, which is why I suggest that it seeks to go beyond hegemony. I argue this because we should recall that hegemony is flexible; it is always contested, always trying to appropriate new elements in order to construct its dominance. In contrast, contemporary forms of imperial power seek to construct closure.

There are of course many other arguments about American power, and some say it is more accurate to describe American imperial power as imperialism. This argument turns on J. A. Hobson's *Imperialism*. Writing at the beginning of the twentieth century, Hobson noted that imperialism meant the conquest of territory and in particular the "method of wholesale partition which assigned to us great tracts of African land." For Hobson, imperialism was marked by "new colonial policy in France and Germany," and the heart of this policy in the case of the British Empire was that no colony established during the late nineteenth century was to be "endowed with responsible self-government."[52] Following this line of argument, some have argued that the American case is one of "imperialism without colonies"[53] or have suggested that America represents a new imperialism. Clearly, the historic trajectory of American power has constructed a language of power in which a form of self-government appears as *the* form of sovereignty.[54] As such, the American imperium is deeply connected to and expresses itself in the political language of liberty and rights. Since the mission of empire is to unfold American liberty, the construction of domination is an important element of American power's repertoire. One important dimension of this process concerns the relationship of American liberalism to power and the intimate connections between political language and its symbolic capacity to do the work of domination. We need to discern as well that imperial power is not simply about either the external deployment of power or foreign policy but is deeply connected to the internal dynamics of power. Imperial power is not only "over there," it is also "over here."

[26]

Liberalism and American Empire

Louis Hartz's *The Liberal Tradition in America* stands as one framing mid-twentieth-century political theory text that attempts to tell the success story of American liberalism. Hartz, inspired by Alexis de Tocqueville's *Democracy in America*, seeks to demonstrate the twentieth-century significance of Tocqueville's nineteenth-century statement about America's uniqueness, by which human beings are born equal "instead of becoming so." For Hartz the consequence of this natural equality was the creation of the liberal mind. In part, Hartz's project found in the uniqueness of America an explanation of why left-wing or socialist movements and ideas could not succeed in America. The historic effect of Hartz's text was to add another component to the success story of American liberalism. Rogers Smith, in his remarkable book *Civic Ideals*, makes the point that in working on American political thought he concluded that neither the Lockean liberalism of Hartz nor the civic republicanism of J. P. Pocock and others adequately explains inequality, race, or American civic identity. Focusing on the meanings of American citizenship, Smith advances a position of "multiple traditions. . . . American political actors have always promoted [these.] [C]ivic ideologies . . . blend liberal, democratic republican and inegalitarian ascriptive elements in various combinations."[55]

Although Smith tries to unearth another tradition which speaks to issues of inequality in America and that demolishes Tocqueville's myth of innate equality, Smith's text does not engage the ways in which liberalism as a set of historic practices might itself be implicated in inequities. Instead, and in a manner typical of conventional, normative, political theory, Smith perceives inequities as alien practices outside of liberalism's frame of reference. These inequities are then explained as gaps between norms and ideals. The political theorist Judith Shklar notes that the emergence over time of a "liberalism of rights" was integral to American liberalism. Observing that the history of American political thought focuses on the idea of rights, she demonstrates that "rights are not this open door that allows us to reach our goals . . . but they allow us to realize our goals *against* others."[56] In other words, liberal practices were simultaneously founded upon a privileging of the individual and the creation of a series of exclusions. It means that *liberalism has a double structure*. When this double structure operates within the crucible of a religious or teleological fate of human destiny, liberalism takes on the mantle of a single truth. One cannot therefore think of American liberalism in purely secular terms. It has to be concretely located within all the discursive frameworks of American thought.

The genealogy of American liberalism is not separate from the founding narratives of the American colonies. For not only did the white settlers flee England either to find a land of religious toleration or to make names for themselves, but they did so as groups that embodied the "rights of Englishmen." These rights were anchored in the rights of conquest and the capacity of the settlers to put aside the rights of the indigenous American population. Richard Hakluyt, in his 1585 text *Pamphlet for the Virginia Enterprise,* describes the situation well when he writes, "We may, if we will proceed with extremity, conquer, fortify, and plant in soils most sweet, most pleasant, most strong, and most fertile, and in the end bring them all in subjection and to civility."[57]

In American thought, readings of liberalism are sometimes connected to the fantasy of virgin lands. This is a fantasy that is deeply embedded in the idea of *res nullius*. William Crashaw, when justifying the Virginia settlement in 1610, preached the doctrine of *res nullius* and urged the settlers forward in a mission to give the "Savages what they needed most, civility for their bodies and Christianity for their souls."[58] The imaginary of virgin lands was one symbolic requirement for the story of American liberalism as the natural unfolding of human destiny. While Donald Pease has made a compelling argument that the rupturing events of September 11, 2001, created a historical turning point in America's entire symbolic apparatus and inaugurated the "Homeland Security State,"[59] the double structure of American liberalism allows us to grasp Pease's apt formulation of the "Homeland Security State" not as an aberration but as one possible, politically logical consequence of the historic practices of liberalism that were operative through an empire of liberty.

In this regard, Sheldon Wolin observed that "the superimposition of empire upon democracy . . . suggests that the traditional categories of citizen, democracy, state, and power desperately need reformulation," and he attempts to do this by positing the idea of the "imperial citizen."[60] It seems to me that the founding moment of America created this citizen, that these qualities were reinscribed by the legalities and materialities of racial slavery, internal territorial expansion, and external interventions, while constructing a version of liberty that would be rooted in the empire of liberty. Today, it is this form of liberty that has become the spectacular embodiment of American imperial power.

The Empire of Liberty and States of Exception

Recent theorization of this moment and of imperial power has been influenced by the writings of Giorgio Agamben and his formulation of "the state of exception."[61] I wish to turn briefly to the ways that political theorists have used Agamben's work. In doing this I critically review the concept of "state of exception" and its applicability to our understanding of American power. American liberalism emerged and developed within and alongside a system of racial slavery, and it is to that system that we now turn in order to review its shaping of American power and the operation of that power. In doing this review, I touch on topics that will be fully developed in the other lectures, but I make a few gestures here to some of these issues, in part to deepen the coherence of the lecture series.[62]

Racial slavery constructed modes of being. As a system of domination and historic injustice, racial slavery and its legacies should force us to think about Theodor Adorno's musings on the possibilities of thinking after Auschwitz. How are we to think after a historical catastrophe? Racial slavery in the United States was based upon what the Caribbean historian Elsa Goveia has called "a special kind of property—that is property in persons."[63] U.S. Supreme Court Chief Justice Roger Taney's opinion in the *Dred Scott* case, which stated that blacks were forms of property, confirms Goveia's analysis. In an astute essay, Colin Dayan notes that "the legal slave [was an] artificial person who [existed] as both human and property." She further argues that "in juxtaposing these two conditions of being . . . the potent image of the servile body can be perpetually invented."[64] The slave codes were illustrative of Goveia and Dayan's view. For example, the slave codes of South Carolina drafted by John Locke stated, "Every Freeman of Carolina shall have absolute power and authority over Negro slaves, of what opinion or religion soever[sic]."[65] Racial slavery meant, in the words of a 1680 Virginia statute, that "if any Negro lift up his hand against any Christian he shall receive thirty lashes, and if he absent himself or lie out from his master's service and resist lawful apprehension he may be killed."[66] So racial slavery created a situation of *civil death*, not just social death as Orlando Patterson argues. It created a legal, ontological, site of the outside, a zone in which the treatment of bodies with violence rested upon laws, customs, and statutes. But this was a problematic outside status, because, although the slave was property, he or she could and did speak. The Cuban poet Nicolás Guillén captures this paradox in his extraordinary poem "I Came on a Slaveship," where we read the following:

> I see Menendez stretched out.
> Immobile, tense
> The open lung bubbles.
> The chest burns.
> His eyes see, are seeing.
> The corpse lives.[67]

This is the paradox: a body that experiences both civil and social deaths, a double death—speaks! It is within this speech that we begin to see the first contours of alternative languages of liberty, now called by the enslaved *freedom*, thereby establishing a series of distinctions that are still in need of explication today.[68]

If, as Michel Foucault notes, the key act of "Sovereign power's effect on life is exercised only when the sovereign can kill. . . . it is essentially the right of the sword,"[69] then it is important to understand how, in racial slavery, the sword of the slaveowner could be wielded. Part of the answer lies in the ways bodies were excluded, and in how these exclusions created the boundaries of the system. The legal exclusion of the slave's black body, the fact that the slave was *property-in-person*, meant that there was an originary, ontological lack of black bodies in the body politic. This created *sites of exceptions* within the polity that were simultaneously intimate with liberal power. It is this intimacy that I think opens another set of doors for analysis.

Within the liberal paradigm, power is supposed to be exercised over "free" individuals, that is, bodies who have a clear field of possible conduct. However, within the *sites of exceptions* (systems of racial slavery and colonialism), there are no free individuals. Power therefore works through violence both as a first and a last resort. But the matter is more complicated than this. Giorgio Agamben, in an analysis of the logic of sovereign power, notes that the exception is outside and what is "outside is included not simply by means of an interdiction or an internment. . . . the exception does not subtract itself from rule; rather the rule, suspending itself, gives rise to the exception and . . . [maintains] itself in relation to the exception."[70] In the systems of racial slavery and colonialism, the exceptions *are the rule.* There is no suspension of any rule to create a new condition of exception. In other words, the close relationship between slavery and the juridical customs and statutes that governed society did not create a figure who can be called *homo sacer.* So in contra-distinction to even critical narratives about liberalism, we find that the regimes of racial and colonial domination mean that liberal practice has a double structure by which it operates. Consequently, there is no gap between norms and ideals, and, contrary to Agamben's position that "the state of exception appears as a threshold of indeterminacy between democracy and absolutism," sites of exceptions as I have described them are themselves constitutive of both historical and contemporary rule.[71] Then there is the matter of how race turns the black body itself into a constituted site of exception. Therefore, even when the black body was legally free (a non-slave), this body could be recaptured and enslaved during slavery. To get a better sense of this, we turn to another aspect of current debate, the discussion about torture and its relation to the notion of cruel and unusual punishment. Again here, we are opening up spaces that we will discuss fully in another lecture.

Abu Ghraib not only opened the door to further criticism of the war in Iraq but punctured the narrative that liberal power does not engage in torture. In addition, the torture of prisoners, detainee abuse at the Guantánamo Bay naval base, and the deployment of certain interrogation procedures force us to reflect upon the practices of liberal power and its double structure. Colin Dayan has pointed out that the history of the notion of "cruel and unusual" has "been coupled in lasting intimacy in our legal language and courts, yet they have been vexed by a persistent rhetorical ambiguity that has been used alternately to protect and to legitimize violence."[72] This ambiguity is embedded in the history of American juridical thought, which had to come to grips with racial slavery and its consequences. For instance, in the 1844 appellate case *Turnipseed v. State*, the chief justice of the Alabama Supreme Court, when overturning the conviction of a slaveowner for beating a slave, noted, "Cruel as indicting the infliction of pain of either mind or body, is a word of most extensive application; yet every cruel punishment is not perhaps unusual; nor perhaps can it be assumed that every common infliction is cruel."[73] But what separates the two? And under what circumstances do "cruel" and "unusual" comingle?

For "cruel" and "unusual" to comingle and operate in tandem, a certain kind of body is required. The slave body was both black and "outside," yet inside the body politic. A similar outside status holds for the prisoners at Abu Ghraib and the "ghost detainees" at Guantánamo Bay. American imperial power has decided that these prisoners and detainees do not fall under the Geneva conventions pertaining to war. Their bodies are not the norm, as any review of the policy debate within the Bush administration reveals. A draft memorandum from the U.S. Justice Department on the application of treaties and laws to detainees argues that the "Taliban militia was more akin to a non-governmental organization that used military force to pursue its religious and political ideology."[74] The document further argues that the Geneva conventions do not apply to what it calls "failed states," since these states are not recognized by international law.[75] The criteria for a failed state are what matter to us here. These include:

- The collapse or near-collapse of state authority
- The prevalence of violence that destabilizes civil society and the economy
- The inability to have normal relationships with other governments[76]

Clearly, these practices represent not just an exception to the norm, not just the suspension of rights, but the use of earlier historical practices in which the following procedures are carried out:

- Construct hierarchical conceptions of the human
- Locate the undeserving outside the body politic
- Render the undeserving civilly dead bodies
- Inflict punishment upon these "dead" bodies

When this is accomplished, torture and cruel punishment are no longer viewed as cruelty, but as techniques of intelligence-gathering.

Judith Shklar has written that "cruelty is a wrong done to another creature." Once liberal power excludes and acts against the human being cruelly, such actions become the painful material assertion of the sovereign and of power.

A second form of exclusion appears in the language of those U.S. Supreme Court cases called the Insular Cases. The cases, tried between 1901 and 1922, laid the discursive framework for the territorial acquisition by the United States of Puerto Rico, Guam, the U.S. Virgin Islands, and American Samoa. In these cases, the language of Justice Edward White extended a series of legal arguments that had emerged during the previous century. Justice White argued that "Puerto Rico was not a foreign country, since it was owned by the United States, it was foreign in a domestic sense."[77] In the 1831 case of *Cherokee Nation v. State of Georgia*, the justices rendered the Cherokees members of "domestic dependent nations."[78] All these exquisite legal formulations of exclusion form, I would argue, an integral part of liberal political practices and thought and are therefore very much part of the liberal archive. And one must remember that these exclusions were also racially organized, making Charles Mills's felicitous phrase *the racial contract* quite apropos.[79] I now turn to the final aspect of the double structure of America's liberalism, the way in which that double structure creates the conditions which transform liberty into a form of domination.

Empire of Liberty, Freedom and Domination

In attempting to describe American liberty, Tocqueville noted that such a liberty "defies analysis . . . it is something that one must feel, and logic has no part in it."[80] In this framework, American liberty was a set of lived experiences whose meanings could only be culled from the experiences themselves. While we are able to glean meanings from our experiences and actions, we can also discern logics. As a speech-act, American liberty functions as a synecdoche for the possibilities and meanings of freedom.

Speech-acts are fundamental to the political. In political practice they can be performative utterances that may function as action itself. In political practice speech-acts not only designate positions but through language create positions, in many instances consolidating themselves both as practice and discourse. However, key social and political ideas are not somehow free-floating and therefore available to be snatched out of the air and made to land wherever one wants. Thus, if we begin to think about how key political terms function in metonymic ways, then we will see that American liberty is not a false ideology but rather one whereby one element of liberty (primarily individual, political liberty) now stands in for liberty itself. Second, and this is important, we need to understand how this form of liberty over time becomes the matrices for political subjectivities.

In the American historical process, as American liberty stood in for liberty in general and became integral to political language, it came to define the entire political field itself. Liberty as speech-act and utterances became constructive of and integral to the creation of legitimacy. I am thinking particularly of how American liberty becomes the idea of America. In this way American liberty as *pax Americana* sets out to achieve what Cicero desired—a "joint community of gods and men," under a single truth.

American liberty has the capacity to act as symbolic power. Pierre Bourdieu makes the cogent argument that "to understand the nature of symbolic power, it is . . . crucial to see that it presupposes a kind of active complicity on the part of those subjected to it."[81] Bourdieu eloquently underscores this observation by noting that "dominated individuals are not passive bodies to which symbolic power is applied, as it were, like a scalpel to a corpse."[8] Since symbolic power acts with consent, the question regarding American liberty is not how consent is manufactured but what are the desires that power seeks to touch and then create. When thinking about the transition from disciplinary power to the new technology of power in the late-eighteenth-century West, Foucault observes that power is directed to "man-as-species," and that "it is therefore not a matter of taking the individual at the level of individuality but, on the contrary, of using overall mechanisms and acting in such a way as to achieve over all states of equilibration or regularity."[83] *Regularity* is the key word here. What American liberty wants to achieve is to become the *regular* and thus normalized political field on which human polity occurs. The political and discursive form by which to do this is the empire of liberty. Such an attempt means that liberty becomes a code for domination, not a metaphor for freedom.

This is perhaps one of the most difficult things for us to grasp: a word that generates feelings of creative human possibilities, that suggests the absence of oppression, now stands as a sign of domination. To work our way through this riddle, we should understand that thought is always embodied. We should also consider that thought has both frames and boundaries and that language and metaphor institute these. Making the case that human life-forms are autoinstituted, Sylvia Wynter argues that human cognition does not represent "an external reality, but rather specif[ies] one." In the realm of the political, this specification was rooted in the problem posed by modern Western theorists of natural liberty. The question was not, what form of government should we have, but how should we be ruled? The shift from absolute sovereign power to representative sovereign power consolidated liberty as the main form of the political. Liberty became linked to naked existence. It was required for security, and, as Graham Burchell observes, by "the end of the eighteenth century, the terms liberty and security have become almost synonymous."[84] Thus, over time liberty as political language and speech-act became embodied in a set of historical practices, not only as a dominant ideology of the powerful, but as what Antonio Gramsci calls the "common sense" of our times, the organizing principle of our ways of life. It is a name that specifies our way of life and has done so for a long time. And today it is the ground from which power seeks to act. As an empire of liberty, power exhibits a drive to flatten all spaces with the smooth language of liberty. It is no wonder that those who are currently enslaved by liberty have mourned its appearance. Perhaps if we begin to think about freedom not as synonymous with liberty but as having a different historical trajectory, as different from Roman liberty and natural liberty, as having emerged from the underside of colonial modernity, we may be able to give a different answer to the new political question, what kind of human beings are we?

My argument here is a simple one. There is a dialectic of freedom that emerges not from the liberal tradition and its double structure but out of the interstices of domination. This practice of freedom disrupts normalized imperial liberty. It is a form of freedom in which there is a poiesis of life with no foreclosures. Such a practice of freedom requires invention and is predicated upon the radical imagination. I will return to the discussion of this form of freedom in the last lecture. For now I wish to leave the last moments of this lecture to the poetry of the African American poet Langston Hughes. He writes:

There are words like *Freedom*
Sweet and wonderful to say
On my heartstrings freedom sings
All day everyday
There are words like *Liberty*
That almost make me cry
If you had known what I know
You would know why.[85]

[2]

RACE, HISTORICAL TRAUMA, AND DEMOCRACY

The Politics of a Historical Wrong

How black men, coming to America in the sixteenth, seventeenth, and eighteenth and nineteenth centuries, became a central thread in the history of the United States, at once a challenge to its democracy and always an important part of its economic history and social development.   —W. E. B. DUBOIS

My job becomes how to rip that veil drawn over "proceedings too terrible to relate." That exercise is also critical for any person who is black, or who belongs to any marginalized category, for, historically, we were seldom invited to participate in the discourse even when we were its topic.   —TONI MORRISON

THIS LECTURE FOLLOWS the one titled "Empire of Liberty: Desire, Power, and the States of Exception" in two ways. First, I continue to explore some of the ways in which contemporary power functions, but this time I pay more attention to issues of race and democracy. In discussing these issues, this lecture works through questions of historical trauma while examining politics and democracy. A second feature of this lecture is the fact that its shape has been generated by our conversations following the first lecture. For this second lecture, I had originally intended to focus on reviewing the relationship between democracy and race, on thinking about how the relationship between the structures of racism and race itself influences discussions and debates about democracy. I would have mostly paid attention to the idea that racial power complicates any idea of democracy, arguing that not much attention has been paid to the issue of complication except in understandings of democracy as a minimalist representation of political equality. As I reflected more upon this issue and upon the question-and-answer period after the last lecture, I became convinced that, with regard to questions of race and democracy today, it would be productive to think about historical trauma, to reflect with you on the ways in which trauma, not as a psychoanalytic term or state, but as a social wound inflicted upon the body and the self, operates within a social context. As I make this move, I pose the following question: what does the process of historical trauma or of an event of historically catastrophic proportions mean when its legacies linger and shape the present? One of the issues this lecture addresses is: how do the processes of historical trauma, not as a single event, but as a historical event of long duration, through repetition become catastrophic, producing conditions and practices in the political realm? From this perspective, I ask: how do these conditions and practices shape democracy? As is my style in approaching these complex issues, I deliver a caveat here. I will not offer a psychoanalytic reading of race and democracy, although I will deploy terms of psychoanalytic provenance. Rather, I will explore trauma and its relationship to racial domination and democracy by working through the original, Greek meaning of the word, trauma as wound, injury inflicted upon a body.

With these preliminary remarks, let us begin. Racial slavery, Jim Crow, and general racial domination pressed down on black human flesh. The performance of power in these circumstances was a form of domination that one may call power *in* the flesh. It was power directing bodies through injury of the flesh. Saidiya Hartman, in a remarkable text on terror and slavery, reminds us that the "terrible spectacle" inducting Frederick Douglass into slavery was the beating of his Aunt Hester.[1] She argues compellingly that the violence inflicted upon the slave body made the slave identify violence as an "original generative act equivalent to the statement 'I was born.'"[2]

If violence is the generative act that creates slave life for the black body, this is a violence upon and in the flesh. Such performances of violence create wounds on the body over a historical period and generate conditions for what we may call a *historically catastrophic* event. Such an event is not a singular one that we mark off with periodization boundaries, including a prelude and an aftermath. Rather, a historically catastrophic event is one in which wounds are repeated over and over again. In the case of coercive racial domination and racial slavery in the Atlantic world, these wounds were repeatable and repeated through the master's whip, rape, shackles, lynching, or the relegation of the slave to the status of a non–human being in everyday life, located, in Frantz Fanon's words, in a "zone of nonbeing."[3] Thus one of my questions is: how can, or rather, how should we think about democracy under such conditions? In this lecture, I am not as interested in how history is written after traumatic events, in grappling with what Dominick LaCapra calls the "elusiveness of the traumatic experience."[4] Instead, I wish to think about *the politics of the wound*, the politics of a historical catastrophe, and the ways in which, if we reflect upon the relationship between the wound as historically catastrophic and as a *wrong*,[5] a different space may open up in which we may talk and think about practices of democracy. From this perspective, democracy is not a consensual, rational practice that operates through forms of deliberative procedures and leaves legacies intact, but is one way to reformulate struggles for forms of radical equality. I wish to open up this political space in part because, if racial domination (either in its coercive form or in twenty-first-century constructions of hegemony) is a site of exception within a racial state, the ending of this form of domination resides in a "constitutive outside." Here I do not mean that the struggles against racial power are simply a dialectical negation of racism. Rather, like all things that are located "outside," radical antiracist practices that have as their logic a radical equality are not commensurate with efforts that focus on racism primarily as the lack of inclusiveness within a democratic polity.

Trauma and History

Let us begin by talking about trauma. Although I am not going to develop a psychoanalytical reading of race and democracy, it is useful to observe some things about trauma at the outset. A lively field of "trauma studies" has opened up in the humanities, due primarily to what can be described as a psychoanalytical turn. One of the leading figures in the field, Cathy Caruth, paraphrases Sigmund Freud when she suggests that in trauma there is a:

> Breach in the mind's experience of time, self and the world—it is not like the wound on the body, a simple healable event, but rather is an event in which the structure of its experience . . . is not assimilated or experienced fully at the time, but rather is only done so, belatedly in its repeated possession.[6]

Another important figure, Ruth Leys, remarks on "the absolute indispensability of the concept [of trauma] for understanding the psychic harms associated with certain central experiences of the twentieth century, crucially the Holocaust but also including other appalling outrages of the kind experienced by the kidnapped children of Uganda."[7] She also notes that today trauma is a "debased currency."[8] Some scholars, when examining the African American experience, have pointed to cultural trauma as one possible way of understanding issues of history and identity. For these scholars, cultural trauma is understood as a "memory accepted and publicly given credence by relevant membership group."[9] In this definition, racial slavery becomes a traumatic event related to memory. I make two observations about this line of argument. First, it takes the view that the experience of trauma is related to flashbacks. Second, it positions collective memory as the source of these flashbacks and recollections. However, most scholars do not address the issue of repeatable wounds that occur because of an initial event. Thus, to see the African American experience primarily in terms of cultural trauma as defined by these scholars does not allow us to grapple with historical trauma as wound. From my perspective, however, memory is a fundamental, contested site of politics and in the case of racial slavery it is of extraordinary importance.

Toni Morrison makes the point that American writing placed a deliberate veil over the event of racial slavery. She notes, "Over and over, the writers pull the narrative short with a phrase such as, 'But let us drop a veil over these proceedings too terrible to relate.'"[10] Morrison's novel *Beloved* rips open this veil as *memory work* becomes storytelling. In *Beloved*, memory work is the recounting of the initial traumatic event and its terrible consequences. The event is too horrible to remember but must be remembered. The politics of such memory work is a complicated matter, but it pushes power to acknowledge a historical wrong. Although Cathy Caruth and others have argued that it is not the experience of the event that causes trauma but the remembering of it, a remembering that occurs after a period of forgetting, the event of racial slavery is of a different character. When describing traumatic neuroses, Freud observes: "Now dreams occurring in traumatic neuroses have the characteristic of repeatedly bringing the patient back into the situation of his accident, a situation from which he wakes up in another fright."[11] As an event, racial slavery was a historical wrong structured around racial domination. Over time two kinds of racial power emerged, one coercive and the other hegemonic. Both in turn generated ways of life that negated the humanness of African Americans.

Racial slavery and its violences constructed what Stephanie Smallwood calls the transformation of "African Captives into Atlantic commodities" and constituted the generative event for the construction of racial domination in the New World.[12] At the level of historical flow, there were two traumatic experiences. The first was the transformation of the African body into an African captive, and the second was an awareness on the part of this captive person of a death that would be experienced differently. Smallwood puts it well when she describes the crossing of the Middle Passage this way: "Entrapped, Africans confronted a dual crisis: the trauma of death, and the inability to respond appropriately to death. . . . more fundamentally, on the sea voyage, even the African dead were enslaved and commodified, trapped in a time–space regime in which they were unable fully to die."[13] The point I am making here is worth repeating. With racial slavery and racial domination there is the repetition of traumatic events. Racial slavery was therefore a layered traumatic event that created the ground and opened up the space for another series of traumatic events that made history a catastrophe, thereby creating a social wound. In such circumstances, trauma as a social wound is experienced, assimilated, and understood immediately by those historically traumatized. There is no temporal gap in the experience. At the same time, this traumatic wound produced an array of politics that constituted critical elements of a black intellectual and political tradition.[14] These elements were in part responses to the historically catastrophic event. However, they did not only work through the event but oftentimes expanded the boundaries of conventional political and social thought.

In drawing a distinction between historical and structural trauma, LaCapra notes that "structural trauma is related to transhistorical absence . . . and appears in different ways in all societies."[15] He argues that this form of trauma is different from historical trauma, which functions in the direction of loss and is "specific, . . . not everyone is subject to it or entitled to it or the subject position associated with it."[16] While we should pay attention to this distinction, the social wound of racial slavery straddles both forms of trauma. Racial slavery generated a historic loss, what Smallwood calls a "disappearance [that] threatened to put saltwater slavery beyond both the physical and metaphysical reach of kin. . . . Would the exiles be able to return home . . . ?"[17] This loss can be grappled with through discourses, politics, and narratives to such an extent that the themes of exodus, redemption, and return litter all the discursive formations of black diasporic politics. This originary loss and exile expressed itself in twentieth-century Ethiopianism as well as in various forms of black internationalism, of which the movement of Marcus Garvey, the Universal Negro Improvement Association (UNIA) was the exemplar in the early part of the last century. The consistent appeal of radical black diasporic movements that embodied conceptions of return arose both from the generative traumatic event and from its repeated repercussions. I put the matter in stark terms: for the African diaspora in the Americas, even if one were not born a slave, the fact of slavery marked one's life. Thus an individual black life becomes lived history, with the historical trauma of racial slavery congealing into wounds and scars of history. One might call these wounds and scars a form of structural trauma.

The wounds and scars of history, when inflicted, are of course witnessed. However, those who witness the wounds do so as outsiders, since the black being is often invisible, or in the words of W. E. B. DuBois, remains "a problem." Often, the witnessing is superficially a blank stare of nonengagement. This is a profound paradox, because, as Robert Gooding-Williams observes in his discussion of DuBois's formulation of American racial domination as the appearance of the "Negro Problem," "Black bodies, in fact, have been saturated with significance."[18] Thus the stare is not one of nonengagement but rather one that already positions the black body as unworthy. The black body was or is, in Fanon's words, marked by "legends, stories, history, and above all historicity."[19] This historicity operates through the repetition of past events and their consistent transformation into wounds. As stated before, racial slavery was the originary trauma; antiblack racism becomes the frame for the repetition of the wound and constructs parallel lives for African Americans. And here I mean two things. First, all major social and economic indices demonstrate that African American lives are adversely impacted in terms of education, income levels, access to health care, and, perhaps most damning of all, incarceration rates for young black men. Glenn Loury makes the point that the prison system in America is the principal venue "in which the legacy of . . . history remains vividly apparent. . . . We are . . . becoming a nation of jailers—and, racist jailers at that."[20] In his Tanner Lectures, Loury accurately argues that substantive racial justice has not been achieved, and he posits that what has occurred is instead a form of "procedural race neutrality." He then remarks that American prisons house 25 percent of the world's inmates and that a large percentage of these individuals are black and brown, in numbers disproportionate to their presence in the population. He observes that a black male resident of the state of California "is more likely to go to state prison than to state college." And Howard Winant makes an important point, which we should ponder. Writing about the new politics of race, he observes that we are in the middle of a transition from "racial domination to racial hegemony."[21] Putting aside my initial concerns about hegemony as a form of domination, I think that Winant is pointing us to the fact that certain forms of coercive domination do not seem as prevalent in what some have called the post–civil rights era as they once were. He also points to the fact that race and racism are constantly being made and remade and are therefore adapted to the demands of the moment.

In addition to social and economic indices (higher rates of unemployment among blacks than whites), there is another dimension to how race is lived in America. I want to turn my attention to a demonstration of how antiblack racism as a structured form of domination reaches out and transforms human relations, becoming the framework within which the social is lived in America. One dominant, common myth in the American narrative is that America is open to all immigrants. I do not wish here to be drawn into current debates about immigration in the United States; my own perspective on the matter mirrors the sentiment on a placard at a demonstration supporting immigrant rights. The placard reads: "No person is a non-citizen." What I wish to draw your attention to is how antiblack racism as a sociohistorical construct operates, structuring and transforming identities.

In 2001 the *New York Times* published a book titled *How Race Is Lived in America*. Built upon numerous interviews and first-person narratives, the text, though not completely successful, offers some glimpses of the everyday meanings of antiblack racism. I wish to draw our attention to one story, because it speaks to the pervasive, dominant constitution of the historicity of the black body as lack.

The story concerns two friends who immigrate to the U.S. from Cuba. In Cuba they were the closest of friends, but in America, Ruiz, one of the two friends, says, "It's like I am here and he is over there . . . and we can't cross over to the other's world." The narrative continues:

> Ruiz discovered a world that neither the American television nor Communist propaganda had prepared him for. Dogs did not growl at him and police officers did not hose him. But he felt the stares of security guards when he entered a store in a white neighborhood and the subtle recoiling of white women when he walked by.[22]

These stares and this recoil are indicative of how the black body, in particular the male black body, is perceived. In 1950, Fanon described a corporeal schema in which the sight of a black body incites fright. He wrote, "'Look, a Negro! . . . Mama, see the Negro! I'm frightened! Frightened! Frightened!'"[23] A half century later, fright turns into stares and recoil, as the black body remains the site of a historical wrong that American democracy has no answer for and is still unable to grapple with. There are many reasons for this, and we will explore some of them in this lecture. One of them has to do with the material privileges of whiteness, which make witnessing a detached experience. As far back as 1903, DuBois put the matter very well when he wrote in *The Souls of Black Folk*, "between me and the other world there is ever an unasked question unasked by some through feelings of delicacy; by others through the difficulty of rightly framing it. All never-the-less, flutter around it."[24] Never fully able to confront the profound meanings of antiblack racism as one consequence of racial slavery, American democracy therefore does not think about the meaning of race for democracy. In part, the problem lies in the narrow liberal conception of democracy as political equality. From this perspective, the way to address racism and its consequences is to work within the framework of a binary of inclusion or exclusion. This way of thinking about race in America evacuates forms of structural legacies, making any analysis of racism reducible to a lack of formal procedural equality that can be solved with different procedures of representation. But the different levels of representation that mark forms of inclusion have not resolved in any way, shape, or form the fact that we are a nation of "racist jailers," making the punishment of prison a form of disciplinary politics for the black body. What is clearly required is another view of democracy, for us to think, if possible, from the perspectives of those who have been slaves, whose ideas and practices have been erased from the body politic. In beginning to do this, I want to engage in a comparative reading of two texts: Alexis de Tocqueville's *Democracy in America* and W. E. B. DuBois's *Black Reconstruction*. I do this as one possible means of beginning to rethink race and democracy in America.

A View of American Democracy

Alexis de Tocqueville's two-volume *Democracy in America* is still seen as the seminal work on American democracy. In the words of Donald Pease, *Democracy in America*, published in 1835, "supplied the concepts, generalizations, and categories out of which U.S. citizens were encouraged to experience and make sense of U.S. democracy."[25] Pease compellingly argues that "political scientists, literary theorists, philosophers, and citizens alike have invested Tocqueville's work with a metahistorical knowingness about U.S. democratic culture."[26] It is therefore appropriate that, in examining American democracy, one begins with Tocqueville's work. In the 1848 edition of the book, Tocqueville wrote that the "advent of democracy as governing power in the world's affairs, universal and irresistible, was at hand." This idea was of course in accord with his original introduction to the book, in which he stated that "the gradual development of the principle of equality is a providential fact."[27] For Tocqueville, democracy in America was about the "general equality of conditions among people."[28] As he made clear in the second volume of *Democracy in America*, equality was a more important political value than political liberty. He notes that "political liberty is easily lost. . . . men therefore hold on to equality not only because it is precious to them; they are also attached to it because they think it will last forever."[29] Tocqueville's preoccupation with democracy was grounded in his sense that a social revolution had broken what he called the "spell of royalty," and this revolution had at its core the principle of equality attached to conditions. This was an equality in which the former hierarchies were threatened. In other words, for Tocqueville the critical question was how a democratic revolution in the nineteenth century could create new conditions, different from those that previously existed. Thus his concern was about more than formal equality; it was about equality as an embedded condition of life. Tocqueville was not as focused on issues of political liberty or political equality as he was on a general condition of equality. We should, however, be clear. It is not that political equality did not matter, because, as Sheldon Wolin has noted, "one of the great themes in *Democracy* is the appearance of the people as full-fledged political actors continuously involved in the exercise of power."[30] However, the "new science of politics" that Tocqueville called for would describe the conditions of equality, conditions under which the so-called "tyranny of the majority" would be more of a cultural force than a legislative force. Tocqueville wondered, as Wolin so ably points out, about "'the invisible and intangible power of thought' affecting millions of beings scattered over vast distances," under these conditions of equality.[31]

I would argue that Tocqueville, when considering these issues and their relationship to democracy, decided that what was necessary was that: "the light of intelligence spreads, and the capacities of all classes tends towards equality. Society becomes democratic, and the *empire of democracy* is slowly and peacefully introduced into institutions and customs" (emphasis mine).[32] Here one should of course note the use of the word *empire*. Wolin has suggested that in this instance it means *sway*. I want to argue that here the word *empire* means the single universal truth under which human beings should live. We know that Tocqueville supported the French colonial empire and that he developed a positive view of French colonialism in his writings on Algeria.[33] In part, his positions on colonialism rested on the popular, conventional concept in European thought that there existed a hierarchy of nations and peoples and that at the apex of this hierarchy were Christian nations, who had a right to civilize so-called "savage nations." Thus I would argue that it was not unusual for Tocqueville to understand democracy as a "providential fact." But what about racial slavery? How did Tocqueville view racial slavery, and how did he see the relationship between slavery and American democracy?

In his 1843 essay "The Emancipation of the Slaves," Tocqueville acknowledged that, regarding the abolition of slavery, "it is difficult to think of greater or more important questions today."[34] He believed that the abolition of slavery was an important issue, because for France the "keeping [of] the colonies is necessary for the strength and greatness of France."[35] For Tocqueville, while abolition was necessary, it had to be achieved under conditions that would not adversely impact French colonialism. Although he did not mention Haiti and the Haitian Revolution in this essay, the memory of the revolution haunted his thinking, particularly when he wrote, "emancipation is . . . A very dangerous enterprise. . . . we must resolve to do it, but at the same time we must study with greatest care the most certain and the most economical means of succeeding."[36] It is therefore safe to say that Tocqueville's attitude toward slavery in the French colonies favored gradual abolition, as long as abolition did not trouble the French colonial enterprise. He saw the system of slavery in the colonies as the foundation of their great wealth. Slavery was integral to the social and economic structure of the colonies and to the sustainability of colonial power. Therefore abolition required a delicate and gradual process. However, when it came to America, Tocqueville had a different view. He did not see racial slavery as integral to the economy of America. His views on slavery were rooted in what he considered to be the natural superiority of white civilization and in the impossibility of blacks and whites' living together.[37] The so-called natural superiority of whites, specifically Anglo-Americans, meant for Tocqueville that, even though black slaves were badly treated as slaves, they were not and could not be part of American democracy. Indeed, from Tocqueville's perspective, racial slavery had no impact upon democracy and the principle of equality. Thus, when Tocqueville turns his attention to questions of race in America at the end of the first volume of *Democracy in America*, he makes it clear that he never had time in the preceding narrative of over three hundred pages to write about slavery, because in his mind slavery was a topic that was "American without being democratic [and] to portray democracy has been my principal aim."[38] For Tocqueville, although slavery was not democratic, it had no relationship to, did not inform, and did not shape American democracy. This is an important point, since such a narrative really argued that racial slavery was somehow separate from American democracy, as opposed to seeing American democracy as based on racial slavery and therefore shaped by its history. This narrative of separation presents slavery as an aberration, not as a historical wrong deeply shaping our present.

It is interesting how Tocqueville finally pays attention to slavery. After hundreds of pages discussing equality as a custom, after many chapters describing some of the political institutions of America (its systems of townships, constitutional arrangements, judicial power, political parties, liberty of the press, various forms of political association, and issues of representative rule by the majority), Tocqueville examines slavery and the genocide of the Native American population not by thinking about these modes of power in their social forms but by taking a distinctly racial view, one in which race is a scientific fact of nature, with some races superior and others inferior. By thinking in this way, Tocqueville could write, without sensing any contradiction, that:

> An absolute and immense democracy is not all that we find in America; the inhabitants of the New World may be considered from more than one point of view. In the course of this work my subject has often led me to speak of Indians and Negroes, but I have never had time to stop in order to show what place these two races occupy in the midst of the *democratic people*. I have shown in what spirit and according to what laws the Anglo-American union was formed[39] (emphasis mine).

We should note here that Tocqueville is very clear—American democracy is racially exclusive, the Anglo-American union is a racial state of white supremacy. It is a racial state that, though democratic, has no need to pay attention to racial slavery and Native American genocide because:

> Among these widely differing families of men, the first that attracts attention, the superior in intelligence, in power, and in enjoyment, is the white, or European, the MAN pre-eminently so called; below him appear the Negro and the Indian. . . . both of them occupy an equally inferior position in the country they inhabit; both suffer from tyranny; and if their wrongs are not the same, they originate from the same author.[40]

Tocqueville then speaks about the oppression of the "Negro," which deprives "the descendents of the Africans of almost all privileges of humanity."[41] Having noted this, he then makes an argument popular at the time, that racial slavery had "debased" the black slave. It was a strange argument. First you make a human being a slave, then you say that his enslavement means that he has become debased and therefore cannot be freed. In this argument, the slave master continues to have his humanity while practicing coercive power over the slave. Debasement, the violence of power *in* the flesh, in the minds of the slave masters and those who witnessed slavery (Tocqueville witnessed slavery in his American travels), created the conditions for the black slave to be a certain kind of creature. Tocqueville writes:

> Equally devoid of wants and of enjoyment, and useless to himself . . . he quietly enjoys all the privileges of debasement. If he becomes free, independence is often felt by him to be an heavier burden than slavery. . . . a thousand new desires beset him, and he has not the knowledge and energy necessary to resist them. . . . In short, he is sunk to such a depth of wretchedness that while servitude brutalizes, liberty destroys him.[42]

Thus for Tocqueville the slave has no capacity to be free even when freed. Brutal oppression has degraded him forever, and the condemned black body is to remain eternally outside of American democracy. But there is for Tocqueville another reason why the black body is condemned to exist outside the framework of American democracy. In an explicit reference to slavery, Tocqueville writes about the black body as follows:

> The modern slave differs from his master not only in his condition but in his origin. You may set the Negro free, but you cannot make him otherwise than an alien to the European. . . . we scarcely acknowledge the common features of humanity in this stranger whom slavery has brought among us. His physiognomy is in our eyes hideous, his understanding weak, his tastes low; and we are almost inclined to look upon him as being an intermediate between man and the brutes.[43]

Tocqueville approvingly cites Thomas Jefferson, who had previously written, "in the book of destiny . . . the two races will never live in a state of equal freedom under the same government."[44] It is clear that American democracy, for all its providential certainty, could not grapple with the consequences of the historical wrong enacted at its inauguration. Thus its answer was to expel the black body. This was not just the view of Jefferson; it was the reason for the formation of the American Colonization Society (ACS) in 1816, founded by Henry Clay and John Randolph, with the membership of Daniel Webster, Busrod Washington (nephew of a Founding Father), George Washington, and James Madison.[45] Many members of the ACS thought that slavery could not be sustained but felt it was impossible for the ex-slave to be integrated into American society. This proposed extraordinary exclusion, permanent if possible, of the black body from the American polity, shaped the character of American democracy.

Another View of American Democracy

If, within the frameworks and canons of American political thought and intellectual history, *Democracy in America* stands as the master text, then W. E. B. DuBois's 1935 book *Black Reconstruction* continues to be ignored. Yet this text forthrightly addresses the foundational issues of American democracy. I do not wish here to engage in any rehabilitative treatment of *Black Reconstruction*. Instead, I want to think through the rich conceptual tools that DuBois uses and in so doing offer some tentative analysis of the present moment and of American democracy.

One hundred years after the first publication of *Democracy in America*, W. E. B. DuBois published *Black Reconstruction in America, 1860–1880*. The book was not widely reviewed at the time, and, as Nikhil Singh has observed, it was criticized for what reviewers saw as its "hyperbolic claims" about the ex-slaves or was "clinically dismantled as a romantic illusion."[46] The Caribbean intellectual C. L. R. James noted that in *Black Reconstruction* the "Negroes *in particular* had tried to carry out ideas that went beyond the prevailing conceptions of bourgeois democracy."[47] If *Democracy in America* was Tocqueville's attempt to think about the democratic revolution in Europe by locating America as the signifier of that revolution (an attempt that allowed him to sidestep the radical democratic movements that appeared in Europe by the 1840s), *Black Reconstruction* was an acknowledgment that, although the 1840s witnessed a radical experiment in democracy in Europe, the black slaves and workers in America had gone beyond even the boundaries of the limits set by antislavery activists. For many antislavery activists the horizon of Reconstruction was black male political equality. The ex-slaves broke this limit. At the end of *Black Reconstruction*, DuBois writes:

> The most magnificent drama in the last thousand years of human history is the transportation of ten million human beings out of the dark beauty their mother continent into the new-found Eldorado of the West. They descended into Hell; and in the third century they arose from the dead, in the finest effort to achieve democracy by the working millions which this world had ever seen.[48]

Some argue, with a degree of accuracy, that *Black Reconstruction* is not part of the canon of American thought because its focus on the self-activities of black slaves does not fit easily into a conventional, national American narrative. I agree, but I would add one thing. *Black Reconstruction* does not fit within the conventional American narrative because it poses the most fundamental questions about American democracy. And in posing these questions, it supplies another language of democracy and its possibilities that is outside our current framework for thinking about democracy. Unlike *Democracy in America*, *Black Reconstruction* makes slavery the central question of American democracy. In the opening sentences of his text, DuBois writes about:

> How black men, coming to America in the sixteenth, seventeenth, eighteenth and nineteenth centuries, became a central thread in the history of the United States, at once a challenge to its democracy and always an important part of its economic history and social development.[49]

For DuBois, American democracy was challenged by the historical wrong of slavery. For him American slavery was "a matter of both race and social condition, but the condition was limited and determined by race."[50] The core of slavery for DuBois was that it "represented in a very real sense the ultimate degradation of man.

Indeed the system was so reactionary, so utterly inconsistent with modern progress. . . . no matter how degraded the factory hand, he is not real estate. The tragedy of the black slave's position was precisely this: his absolute subjection to the individual will of an owner."[51]

Racial slavery was about the degradation of the human being. As a system of "property in the person," it represented the ultimate form of domination. For such a system to exist alongside American democracy was not a gap between reality and ideal, a gap that could then be overcome by a series of inclusionary practices, bringing formal equality to those to whom it had been denied. Rather, an entirely new conception of democracy was required. So what would this democracy look like and how would we name it? But we should not run ahead of our narrative; let us see how DuBois begins to clear a new space in which we may think about American democracy.

At the beginning of his text, DuBois makes the case for us to begin rethinking the category of the slave. He argues that the wealth of the United States and indeed of the Atlantic world was created by slave labor on plantations that were the most modern productive machines of the period. The important historical point here is not the one made by Eric Williams in his book *Capitalism and Slavery*, about the centrality of black slave labor to the process of capitalist accumulation. Rather, DuBois is making a point about slaves as a human social category. By calling the slaves black workers, DuBois shifts two framing assumptions. He changes our conceptions of modernity and creates grounds for the slaves to invent their own forms of lives wherever possible. In his classic work on the Haitian Revolution titled *The Black Jacobins*, C. L. R. James had performed a similar process of naming, making the point that: "The slaves worked on the land, and, like revolutionary peasants everywhere, they aimed at the extermination of their oppressors. But working and living together in gangs of hundreds on the huge sugar-factories which covered the North Plain, they were closer to a modern proletariat than any group of workers in existence at the time."[52] In other words, when one considers the writing of history from the vantage point of those excluded from society, those who, in the words of Jacques Rancière, constitute "a part of those who have no part,"[53] the question of naming, of the creation of new categories, becomes a central element of that writing.

Throughout *Black Reconstruction*, DuBois draws us into the life of these black workers or slaves, so that by the time they begin joining the Union Army, it is obvious that they are involved in what he calls a "general strike." DuBois writes about the mass movement as the war unfolds of black slaves or workers into the Union Army in this way:

> This was merely the desire to stop work. It was a strike on a wide basis against the conditions of work. It was a general strike that involved directly in the end perhaps a half million people. They wanted to stop the economy of the plantation system, and to do that they left the plantation system.[54]

But the black slave or worker had another objective: freedom. In the most lyrical chapter of his book, one that produces a poetic and historical knowledge of the conceptions of the slaves or workers of freedom from the absolute domination of slavery, DuBois attempts to produce what has been a special feature of radical black writing. He reaches for the interiority of the ordinary slave and then represents that interiority as a form of knowledge. In this part of the text, DuBois attempts to find both language and speech utterances that represent a rupture. He titles the chapter "The Coming of the Lord." DuBois presents to us the freedom of the slaves in the poetic language of African American religious practices. He writes:

> The mass of the slaves, even the more intelligent ones, and certainly the great group of field hands, were in a religious and hysterical fervor. This was the coming of the Lord. This was the fulfillment of prophecy and legend. It was the Golden Dawn, after chains of a thousand years. It was everything miraculous and perfect and promising. For the first time in their life, they could travel; they could see;

they could change the dead level of their labor; they could talk to friends and sit at sundown and in the moonlight, listening and imparting wonder-tales. . . . and above all they could stand up and assert themselves. They need not fear the patrol; they need not even cringe before a white face, and touch their hats. . . . Then in addition . . . they wanted to know . . . they were consumed with the desire for schools. The uprising of the black man, and the pouring of himself into organized effort for education in those years between 1861 and 1872, was one of the marvelous occurrences of the modern world.[55]

Here DuBois is describing a radical process that begins to unfold in American history, one that opens up another space for conceptions of democracy. The American Revolution established a limited, male, representative, democratic system, and, as I have made clear in the first lecture, because of racial slavery that revolution could only invest the meaning of liberty with the narrow freight of political liberty and political equality for white males.

When writing about revolution, Hannah Arendt makes two points that we might do well to remember. The first point is that "revolutions are the only political events which confront us directly and inevitably with the problem of beginning."[56] The question we should ask is, was the American Revolution a new beginning? We should ask this question in part because of Arendt's second point: "[W]ho could deny the enormous role the social question has come to play in all revolutions?"[57] If the social was placed outside the framework of the American Revolution and the Revolution's focus was on the political realm, then what kind of revolution was the American Revolution? This is a complex question, and I will not pretend to develop an answer in this lecture. I just wish to pose it because there were two central questions during the American Revolution: racial slavery and colonial domination. That the Revolution answered one and not the other opened up a political logic that culminated in the Civil War. Even Arendt does not see this political logic, the logic of *the politics of the wound*. She tellingly writes that the reason for the success of the American Revolution was "that the predicament of poverty was absent from the American scene. . . . They [the revolutionaries] were not driven by want, and the revolution was not overwhelmed by them [problems of poverty]. The problem they posed was not social but political."[58] In reference to racial slavery, Arendt states that, although there was an obvious "incompatibility of the institution of slavery with the foundation of freedom," the major figures of the American Revolution were indifferent toward slavery. In Arendt's mind, this indifference was caused "by slavery rather than on any dominance of self-interest."[59] This is of course quite a paradox, which Arendt did not face, in part because she wanted to demonstrate that the success of revolutions in general remains in the political domain and that their failures are linked to preoccupations with the social. However, for the black slaves or workers there could be no separation of the social from the political. They were not completing the American Revolution during the period of radical Reconstruction. Instead, they were opening up a political space in which democracy, freedom, and equality would have a new relationship and meaning. They were empirically engaged with the "problem of the new beginning." They were attempting a different revolution.

Before finding a language for describing this event, DuBois tells us, in perhaps the most moving passage of *Black Reconstruction*, that: "The magnificent trumpet tones of Hebrew Scripture, transmuted and oddly changed, became a strange new gospel. All that was Beauty, all that was Love, all that was Truth, stood on the top of these mad moorings and sang with the stars. A great human sob shrieked in the wind, and tossed it tears upon the sea,—free, free, free."[60] What DuBois is pointing us to is this. All historically catastrophic events, while wounding, produce cries. In hearing and listening to these cries we begin to glimpse alternative possibilities in relation to the historically catastrophic event. With these glimpses, a society may begin to work through its history and construct a polity that takes account of this history. This working through concerns not only acts of atonement and forgiveness but also enactments of radical transformation. Continuing in the language of the transmuted Hebrew Bible, DuBois tells us that with the emancipation of the slaves, "the nation was to be purged of continual sin." The tragedy in DuBois's mind is that this process was defeated and America continued its march onward, continuously transforming liberty into imperial freedom. So now, what was the name of the new democracy that was possible? And how does this name help us to think about American democracy?

Abolition Democracy

For DuBois the chief significance "of slavery in the United States to the whole social development of America lay in the ultimate relation of slaves to democracy."[61] DuBois sees this relationship as one that included issues of labor, property ownership, the right to vote, and education. When describing the aftermath of the Civil War, DuBois suggests that two theories of America clashed at that time. In the epigraph to chapter 7, he writes the following: "How two theories of the future of America clashed and blended after the Civil War: the one was abolition-democracy based on freedom, intelligence and power for all men; the other was industry for private profit directed by an autocracy determined at any price to amass wealth and power."[62] DuBois identifies *abolition democracy* as the combination of three distinct streams in American thought and political history. One stream was the transformation of "Puritan Idealism into a theory of universal democracy . . . expressed by the Abolitionists," along with some labor leaders of the period and those DuBois calls "leaders of the common people like Thaddeus Stephens."[63] There are three elements of abolition democracy that DuBois has in mind and that define it. These are the drive to end racial slavery, the positioning of labor as a democratizing force in industrial production, and a general commitment to ordinary people and their aspirations.

This perspective on the political meaning of abolition democracy at once broadens the realms in which equality must now operate. Not only is there full procedural equality between the ex-slave, the ex-master, and the rest of the population, but this equality democratizes economic production and opens up a space for the political speech acts of the ordinary person. DuBois argues that over time abolition democracy was pushed "towards the conception of a dictatorship of labor, although few of its advocates wholly grasped the fact that this necessarily involved dictatorship by labor over capital and industry."[64] Some critics argue that, because DuBois was obviously influenced by Marxist theory at this stage of his life and was working through it, his conception of the dictatorship of labor is ill defined, particularly since, in the chapters on South Carolina, Mississippi, and Louisiana, he depicts a black proletariat that establishes a quasi-dictatorship of labor. However, I would suggest a different possible interpretation. We know that in the 1930s, DuBois, though interested in Marxist theory, also felt that Marxism was not the full answer to the issues of racial domination and class exploitation of African Americans. In 1933, two years before the publication of *Black Reconstruction*, he had already written an article titled "Marxism and the Negro Problem," in which he stated that although Marxism was a "true diagnosis of the situation in Europe . . . it must be modified in the United States of America and especially so far as the Negro group is concerned."[65] In *Black Reconstruction*, DuBois attempts these modifications, forcing us to construct a set of possible new grounds for thinking about the significance of racial slavery to America and also providing us with possible language for thinking about American democracy.

It seems to me that the concept of *abolition democracy* might provide us today with the political language to move past conventional notions of the relationship of democracy to political equality. In order to probe this further, let us leave DuBois for a while and briefly review the term democracy and some of its political meanings.

Democracy

In conventional narratives about Western political thought and philosophy, the concept of democracy begins in Athens. As John Dunn has demonstrated, "from the days of Pericles to those of Demosthenes a full century later [democracy] was a system of citizen self-rule."[66] What is important and often left out in narratives of Western democracy is that Pericles' funeral oration, given to us by Thucydides in *The History of the Peloponnesian War*, was about freedom. In other words, citizen self-rule is intimately linked to a conception of freedom.[67] I think we need to be reminded of this, because over time democracy has shifted away from this relationship and has become primarily a procedure of government. If, within Western thought, Pericles offered democracy as a way of life when he declared that "freedom is typical of life in our community," then John Dewey's statement of 1885 that "democracy is a form of government only because it is a form of moral and spiritual association," though it attempts to retrieve democracy as a way of life, neglects to add freedom to this mix. I would argue that over time the issues of slavery and other forms of servitude complicated democracy in Western thought, and, when it began to reappear as a demand in the seventeenth century, democracy required two things. The first was a form of equality that could be realized through a system of representative government. The second was, as Rancière claimed, that democracy became invested with the notion of a "community of equals," a radical demand for equality. Given this history, while I generally agree with Ernesto Laclau that democracy functions as a horizon "which establishes, at one and the same time, the limits and terrain of the constitution of any possible object,"[68] it seems to me that in politics these limits are established by a series of specific actions and demands at a given historical moment. Democracy may be an empty signifier, but it is one that is filled at each moment. Thus, while there is no transhistorical meaning to the term, it has precise meanings at specific junctures. However, our interest in this lecture is in the question of democracy and representation.

During the period of colonial modernity, the question of representation emerged in England with the Levellers and the Putney Debates. These debates, as C. L. R. James makes clear, are a rich source of ideas about the practice of a democratic politics; however, I want to focus on how the question of the relationship between representation and politics was posed. In the document "An Agreement of the People," the Levellers stated that peace could only be established "upon the grounds of common right and freedom."[69] Upon this freedom they propose that "the people do of course choose themselves a Parliament once in two years. . . . And that the power of this and all future representatives of this nation is inferior only to those who choose them."[70] It is obvious that the concept of representation, as an alternative to self-rule, was influenced by the emergence of the modern state and by the idea of sovereignty and natural rights that could be representative and represented. In other words, political representation was located elsewhere, outside of common, daily life, but reflected the common community. In such a context equality divided itself up, with one element becoming political equality. Now the issue of representation in general is an interesting one. When we think about representation, we typically consider questions of culture, language, and the way in which meaning is produced. Stuart Hall argues that there are two types of systems of representation. He says that the first

> enables us to give meaning to the world by constructing a set of correspondences or a chain of equivalences between things—people, objects, events, abstract ideas etc. . . . [and] the second depends on constructing a set of correspondences between our conceptual map and a set of signs, arranged or organized into various languages which stand for or represent those concepts.[71]

Regarding representative democracy that moves beyond a system of procedural governance, such a framework of democracy at first blush might mean assembling a community. However, representative democracy does not organize a series of correspondences in a conceptual political field. Instead, it inserts a break, divorcing politics from action, from community, and, in the end, from equality. It does this in two ways. In the first, it reduces politics and democracy to the right of formal political equality. Secondly, it constitutes the processes of representation within the symbolic world of institutions (what Cornelius Castoriadis calls the second-order symbolic network) as an empty sign. This empty sign, however, has the capacity to do work because at the level of politics its language is about a relationship and an expression of the social, while that language simultaneously obscures the social. Thus the work of representation in liberal representative democracy is to confirm a series of slippages that make democracy a gap. Inside that gap, there is no political speech-act of the many. In American democracy, this gap is filled by a series of representations that have operated after the 1960s civil rights movement within a narrative of inclusion.

Any serious reading of what has been called the civil rights movement of mid-twentieth-century America indicates that this movement was multilayered and that different political currents existed within it. One current demanded a version of rights that went beyond political and civil rights and sought a complete overhauling of American society. This current, represented by the ideas and work of Martin Luther King, Jr., in his later years and by the work of the Student Nonviolent Coordinating Committee (SNCC) and Ella Baker, was a drive for freedom. At its core was a conception of freedom that bundled together all rights, along with a desire to find a new basis for living in what Martin Luther King, Jr., called the "beloved community." There was also another current, which focused its energies on inclusion and representation. Simply put, there have always been different currents in African American political thought and life, including those who advocated integration with the system and those who felt, in the words of Ella Baker, that "by and large [the movement] had a destined date with freedom . . . not limited to a desire for personal freedom or even freedom for the Negro in the South. It was repeatedly emphasized that the movement was concerned with *the moral implications of racial discrimination for the whole world and the human race*"[72] (emphasis mine).

What is the importance of this to the issues we began with, historical trauma, race, and democracy? For those individuals and groups for whom integration was the primary objective and goal, representation became the crucial move. However, to enter into the "political kingdom" in this way required forgetting the historical wrong or developing a narrative of the historical wrong as a past event. Thus, representation as integration required establishing the historical wrong as a narrative of historical significance but one with little contemporary meaning for politics and democracy. In this universe, black representation becomes a way to forget the historical wrong. Such forms of representation (that is, of representation as only integration) remove themselves from the cries of the wound, because from this perspective the wound has been healed or is healing. In such a context American democracy continues to neglect its founding historical wrong as well as the consequences of that wrong.

So what is or can be the relationship between democracy and a historical wrong? I will offer only the following thoughts. In the first place, we know that one requirement of politics is speech. For American democracy to be transformed, one central element of speech must be the full recognition of the historical wrong of the nation's founding, not as an aberration but as an event constitutive of the inaugural event itself. Thus the historical wrong is not an event that can be discarded or placed in a memory box and then erased. Speaking of this historical wrong raises issues of freedom and equality. And here the question is, how does one constitute a community of equals? At this point, we have to reengage with the ethos and practices that pervade *Black Reconstruction* rather than those of

Democracy in America. There is a radical equality in *Black Reconstruction* that is missing from *Democracy in America*, not only because of the latter's racial silences and assumptions of a racial hierarchy among humans, but because the equality of Tocqueville is not one that is worked through daily, which is invented and reinvented and which then encompasses the social. One may ask, on what grounds can such an equality, one that is beyond political equality and that takes into account the social, be built? My suggestion is a simple one. It can only be built on the common ground that we are all human. But for the community to hold in common the fact that we are all human as a principle of fraternity and solidarity and therefore as the basis of politics, we will have to return to the cries of "free, free, free," that DuBois writes so poetically about. Jacques Rancière argues that democracy is neither a "compromise between interests nor the formation of a common will."[73] Democracy is about dialogue, he argues, but dialogue must be heard to be effective, and to be heard it must be a dialogue of equals. If radical politics begins with the demand of "the part of no part," then transforming American democracy requires working through the politics of the wound of racial slavery and racial domination, not as a historical memory but as a present past, while taking heed of what the cries of freedom may mean for any project of human emancipation. In the end, the current form of American democracy is integral to the domestic political guise of the empire of liberty. Standing on the platform of the cries of freedom, we begin not to create liberty trees but to construct ways of life that make us human.

[3]

DEATH, POWER, VIOLENCE, AND NEW SOVEREIGNTIES

Do not be deceived by the multiplicity of sounds that ring and jingle like laughter. . . . Death speaks with a thousand whispers, but a single voice.   —ROGER MAIS

We must complete our life before our death.   —MICHEL FOUCAULT

If any detainee refused to comply with a lawful order to weed, the plan was that two warders should be allocated to that detainee and, by holding his hands, physically make him pull weeds from the ground . . . once such token work had been performed by the detainee he would have considered that he had broke his Mau Mau oath which had, by superstitious dread, previously prevented him from cooperating.
   —REPORT OF THE COMMITTEE TO INVESTIGATE DISCIPLINARY
   CHARGES AGAINST OFFICERS OF THE KENYA PRISON SERVICE

I WANT TO THANK all of you for coming, particularly those of you who have been following the series. We can now safely say that one of the critical questions that these lectures continue to focus on is what one may call the constituting of subjectivities. To keep the various threads of these lectures clear, I want to quickly draw some connections between the first two lectures and this one. I have been arguing that in our present moment empire as power has established a trajectory in which it seeks to become a totality. Part of empire's drive today is to capture desire in order to create a political field of regularity for our subjectivities. From within the framework of this drive, self-regulation functions as a form of domination.

This self-regulation is integral to what I will describe as the political field of regularity, which occurs under the sign of *freedom*. This freedom is typically called *liberty*, and so I have argued that we currently live under a configuration of power that operates as an *empire of liberty*.

My second major thesis has been about the possibility of democracy's being an empty signifier and how sometimes it has been conceptualized as lack and an entity that must be filled. In this regard democracy becomes a series of prefixes that then define what is being fulfilled (representative democracy, direct democracy, and so on). Focusing on American democracy, I have argued that the social structures of racial slavery as historical wound mean that the story of democracy told by Tocqueville in *Democracy in America* is woefully inadequate. Instead I have suggested that W. E. B. DuBois's *Black Reconstruction* offers a richer and more productive account of the possibilities of democracy in America, not only because he pays attention to slavery but because he makes an attempt to unearth historical knowledge of the slave's understanding and practices of freedom. This attempt opens up a different narrative of democracy and its relationship to freedom, suggesting another form of democracy that DuBois called *abolition democracy*. It is of course critical to my main argument to note that democracy is an important element of the empire of liberty. However, this is a democracy of political equality and voting, a democracy that constitutes itself as a form of political life that we may call *constitutional representativeness*.

In the second lecture, I also began to turn to the body. With this third lecture, I wish to foreground this concern. If the empire of liberty operates through signs of democracy and liberty within a political field of regularity, it has not abandoned violence. Hence in this lecture I want to pay some attention to this matter. I will be doing so from three perspectives. First, I pay some attention to issues of genocide. Second, I look at the question of torture and its possible relationship to the empire of liberty. Then in the final segment, I make an ethnographic shift to review the practices of violence in the postcolonial space of Jamaica, and I leave behind a bit of my preoccupation with empire. I make this detour because the question of violence is a complex one and should be examined from many angles. All three of the topics that I review are different in many ways, but, by looking at them together, I seek to understand violence not simply as an action of instrumentality, nor as a practice that works through a means-end logic, but as one face of power that in some instances becomes power itself. Having presented a map of this sort, let me open my reflections with a few remarks on the most spectacular kind of violence, genocide.

Genocide

We know that the term genocide was coined in 1944 by Raphael Lemkin from the Latin *genos-cide*. Translated, it means the killing of a race. Genocide is about the systematic deployment of death as perpetual motion. As an interview with one of the killers in the Rwandan genocide makes clear: "During that killing season we rose earlier than usual, to eat lot of meat, and we went up to the soccer field at around nine or ten o'clock. The leaders would grumble about latecomers, and we would go off on the attack. Rule number one was to kill. There was no rule number two. It was an organization without complications."[1] Conventionally defined as the systematic killing of a race, genocide entails actions calculated to bring about the physical destruction of the entirety of or a significant section of an identifiable human population. Genocidal actions are not random acts of violence, and they require political organization, mobilization, and ideological justification. In other words, there are always political objectives involved in genocide, including the creation of an order in which a so-called other is murdered and thus bodily expelled from the polity. When thinking about the emergence of the word *genocide*, we should note that Lemkin regarded genocide as connected to colonialism.[2] There are many reasons for this. One is of course that colonial power operates by physically removing human populations, murdering large groups and construct-ing racial hierarchies. Colonial power was always about race and space, and colonialism was embedded within the framework of a racial, biologistic conception of world history in which some human populations were not necessary for the survival of the fittest or for civilization. Those unsuitable could be, and were, expelled from the polity or might remain as inferior beings dominated by those con-sidered civilized. Hannah Arendt makes the point that genocide as-sumes that some human beings are superfluous. We have noted that this assumption has its source in Europe's colonial past, making the idea of superfluousness one of the ideological justifications neces-sary for genocide. In the past century, the world has witnessed many genocides, including the 1904 genocide of the Herero people in the nation-state of Nambia by colonialist Germany, the Armenian geno-cide occurring from 1915 through 1918, the Holocaust, and the Rwandan genocide of 1994. In this lecture, I am not going to focus on each of these genocidal events; instead, I wish to pay some at-tention to a few thinkers who have reflected on the relationship between genocide and power.

For Hannah Arendt, the event of genocide occurs in conditions under which power is attempting to exercise itself as a totality. She makes the additional point that genocide occurs when power seeks to eradicate human plurality. Arendt notes that genocide is about trying to create the conditions for "a total explanation of the past, total knowledge of the present and total and absolute predication for the future."[3] In this drive for totality, there is slippage and even-tual collapse of the distinctions between history and nature. The result is a fusion of the laws of history and the laws of nature into a unitary movement.

It is this drive for totality that interests us. What are its features and how does it reproduce itself into violence and the making of death? Genocide requires spectacle, and even though we may find this difficult to grasp, it also needs mass participation, even if the individuals who engage in genocidal activity act out of fear for their own lives.[4] And here the participation is at two levels. The first level requires the tacit support of significant segments of the population, particularly when genocidal action is actively carried out by a specially created group or in designated locations. The second level occurs when significant segments of the population themselves become killers. As difficult as it is for us to contemplate, given our moral antipathy to genocide, it is within the spectacle of violence enacted through genocide that we begin to understand death as a flow and the creation of death-worlds. Therefore, even though violence and in particular genocidal violence seem to exist beyond the human imagination and, sometimes, beyond our comprehension, we have an obligation, in the words of Susan Sontag, to "take in what human beings are capable of doing to one another."[5]

As we think about genocide, and thinking about genocide is something we must do, let us spend some time with the statement of the general who was responsible for the Herero genocide. When discussing his methods and rationale for this genocide, General Lothar von Trotha, the key figure of the genocidal campaign, stated, "The exercise of violence with crass terrorism and even with gruesome murders is my policy. I destroy the African tribes with streams of blood and streams of money. Only following this cleansing can something new emerge, which will remain."[6] What General Trotha stated with stark clarity is that genocidal violence is about cleansing, the creation of an order based on a notion of purity. Whether it is the extermination of an ethnic group or a religious group, the purpose is to cleanse the social body. In order to do this, the social order to be purified must have within it a population that can be killed with ideological legitimacy. So there are now two things that we should reflect on for a while.

Foucault tells us that historically sovereign power exercised its sovereignty through a right over life. He notes also that when, in nineteenth-century Europe, this right was transformed into the right to "make live and let die," it still belonged to the sovereign. What genocidal violence does is to *disperse* that right over life. It is true

that genocidal violence is done on command and is therefore organized, but its logic is to create the conditions under which murder
becomes a legitimate form of activity and a new world of death can
be constructed. This new death-world is partly constructed by the
state that organizes the genocide but also assumes a different legitimacy when murder is enacted by the significant segments of a population. Listen again to an interview with a Rwandan killer: "The
intimidators made the plans and whipped up enthusiasm; the shop-
keepers paid and provided transportation; the farmers prowled and
pillaged. For the killings, though, everybody had to show up blade
in hand and pitch in for a decent stretch of work."[7] Killing now
becomes a day of work. It is viewed as part of an everyday fact of
life within what was called in Rwanda the "killing season."

Arendt, in her report on the Eichmann trial, pays attention to
the ordinariness of Eichmann. She writes that despite all the efforts
of the prosecution, "everybody could see that this man was not
a 'monster,' but it was difficult indeed not to suspect that he was
a clown."[8] When killing becomes ordinary work, the "banality of
evil" is established. These two cases, which we have briefly referred
to here, one of a quasi–state official and the other of an ordinary
subject, demonstrate the ways in which murder becomes ordinary.
And, as always is the case at the level of action, language is central
to making death and murder everyday realities. Again we listen to
a Rwandan who participated in the genocide: "We had to work
fast, and we got no time off, especially not Sundays—we had to fin-
ish up. We cancelled all ceremonies. Everyone was hired at the same
level for a single job—to crush all the cockroaches."[9] Cockroaches,
this was the name given to the Tutsis. This was the marker that
made them different, less than human. We should also note that the
speaker does not talk about killing cockroaches but instead about
crushing cockroaches, evoking a different image. One crushes a
cockroach as an insect, to get rid of it, to clean one's house of possible contamination. Here language is used to mask murder, as acts
of genocide become work. The substitution and masking operating

here are important in the creation of a legitimate death-world for those enacting murder.

When writing about the Holocaust, Arendt details the processes by which it was enacted. She writes:

> Last came the death factories—and they all died together, the young and the old, the weak and the strong, the sick and the healthy; not as people, not as men and women, children and adults . . . not as good and bad, beautiful and ugly—but brought down to the lowest common denominator of organic life itself, plunged into the darkest abyss of primal equality, like cattle, like matter, like things that had neither body nor soul, nor even a physiognomy upon which death could stamp its seal.[10]

The violence of genocide is performed by creating conditions in which death is absolute. There is no redeeming feature to death for those who die by genocidal violence. Some time ago, Franz Kafka made the point that "death and only death" gives meaning to life. But genocidal death is a death whose finality is of one who has no life. Thus, while at many funerals we speak of the life of the deceased in a ritual that marks life, and then we mourn, in the death of genocidal violence there is no life to mark, since all life has been erased to create the conditions of the violence. For those murdered in what Primo Levi calls "gigantic death machines,"[11] death is the final act in a subject's inability to be, while for those who enact the death chamber or the killing season, death by genocidal violence is about purification. Levi writes, "Even the manner of killing (chosen after careful experiment) was openly symbolic. The gas prescribed and used was the same used for disinfecting ships' holds and sites invaded by bugs or lice."[12] In this process of purification through the creation of a death-world, new boundaries are created and maintained by terror. Arendt compellingly suggests that genocidal violence is integral to totalitarian terror. However, this terror is often not outside the law but functions inside it and is given legitimacy as authorized death.

So how do we grapple with genocidal violence and its relationship to power? Regarding violence, Arendt makes the point that violence is the opposite of power. She notes further that when "violence appears, power is in jeopardy."[13] Splitting power and violence into two distinct entities, Arendt argues that although they are distinct, "they usually appear together." Here Arendt is working with a conception of power in which political authority has a legitimate monopoly on force. In this paradigm, violence is an instrument that follows a means-end logic. However, what happens when this kind of violence is not only an instrument but an integral part of a regime of rule, when death and terror (not fear) become the singularity of power? What happens when death is not the means-end but the actual process itself? Or to put this another way, what happens when power operates as surplus power in a mode of regular consistency, when violence and death are not interruptions of routine but are themselves the routine? In such situations, there is no gap between means and ends. Violence does not become an expression of power but takes on the mantle of power itself. I would argue that the event of genocidal violence and the colonial project practice violence as power in similar ways. For the former, the performance of power as violence has historically been of relatively short duration, while for the latter, power as might as right, power as the sword, operates historically over a longer time frame. The matter of temporality is important, but not as a means of comparison of relative oppression, of deciding which system or event was more evil. (Such a discussion has no real meaning or substance. On what basis do we compare piles of dead bodies?) Instead, when thinking about the sword of colonial power and about genocidal violence, we need to examine how technologies of violence are codified, reappear, and repeat themselves.

When Hannah Arendt critiques Frantz Fanon on the issue of violence, she fails to recognize that certain kinds of violence collapse into power. Arendt's reading of Fanon's chapter on violence in *The Wretched of the Earth* is superficial because she argues that Fanon agrees with "glorified violence for violence' sake."[14] Any serious reading of Fanon suggests that this is not so, but that is not the point of this lecture. Rather, regarding Arendt's assessment of Fanon, I suggest that what was at work in her thought was the absence of the body as a possible site within the political field. At the sites where violence operates as power, not only is death perpetual motion, but the regular crushing of life from the body becomes the crushing of animated life. Thus death has a political purpose when it becomes the ultimate negative ground of the human. To put this another way, a regime of extreme violence has to enact regular practices of death because its purpose is the absolute negation of the human life-form in its plurality. The killing of the body, whether in the intimate spaces of the villages of Rwanda or in the death camps of the Nazis, makes the body upon which death is visited a materiality and a surface, confirming what Mary Douglas makes clear, that there is no "body that does not involve at the time a social dimension."[15]

I would argue, therefore, that because of this social dimension, Foucault's statement that the "body is also directly involved in a political field" is accurate. Elaine Scarry makes the same point about pain and torture. She observes that "it is the intense pain that destroys a person's self and world."[16] Thus, when power acts upon the body, the primary aims of torture are to destroy the "meaning-making capacity of the tortured and . . . to replace it with the meanings of the torturer."[17] Thus the body as animated life becomes an object to be seized and mastered. Regimes of extreme violence dominate through a form of power that operates in the flesh.

Let me summarize my main argument before I move on to the issue of torture. I have suggested an interpretation in which violence is not an instrument of power but instead, in extreme regimes (for example, a state that practices genocide), is a form of power that itself creates a death-world. This is of course a different conception from that found in the conventional social science literature on the subject. In this literature, beginning with the work of Max

Weber, a preoccupation with power centers on notions of political authority, political obligation, and a command-obedience model, or, as in the work of Talcott Parsons and others, on power as a "specific mechanism operating to bring about changes . . . in the processes of social interaction."[18]

Michel Foucault disrupts these conceptions of power and argues that it may be productive to ask "What happens?" in order to "undertake a critical investigation of the thematics of power."[19] By asking how power is exercised in contexts of extreme regimes, I have posited the possibility that violence, particularly genocidal violence, is power. Of course this position runs counter to Foucault's position, since he makes a distinction between a relationship of violence and one of power, which he says "bends, it breaks, it destroys, or closes off all possibilities."[20] For Foucault the capacity of power is based upon a relationship in which a subject emerges. His is an attempt to understand the liberal project. On the other hand, I wish to suggest that bending, breaking, destroying, and closing off all possibilities also demand a certain kind of relationship, one in which total domination through force is an objective. In this regard, it is important to remember that one way to examine power is not to separate its methods and actions from its outcomes. Here I am not speaking about intent but rather about practices. It is through these lenses that I have suggested another way to think about the relationship between violence and power.

Second, I have also argued that one objective of this kind of power is to create a political order based upon purification. Third, I have suggested, as have Arendt and others, that the technologies of genocidal violence are to be found in colonial power. We need to begin to see and think about genocidal violence, as unthinkable as it is and as difficult as it may be to contemplate, in order to find language to describe how it operates as a form of power that is not an aberration but one possible, logical consequence of power that can be deployed on the body by crushing it. Let me now turn to the issue of torture and to contemporary features of an empire of liberty.

Torture and Violence

In 1982 the liberal political theorist Judith Shklar posited that cruelty was "irrevocably" the first vice.[21] She noted that "cruelty as the willful inflicting of physical pain on a weaker being in order to cause anguish and pain . . . is a wrong done entirely to *another creature*"[22] (emphasis in original). Shklar then suggested that one element of liberalism was its avoidance of cruelty. Since the onset of the so-called war on terror, the issue of an extreme form of systematic cruelty—torture—has opened up a series of discussions and debates. In the debate, one line of thinking has emerged that has forcefully argued for the necessity of "dirty hands."[23] The central assumption of this argument is the idea of the ticking bomb. Put simply, this idea holds that the extraction of information and necessary intelligence in order to avert a disaster might require methods of torture. David Luban has pointed to a liberal theory of torture in which the argument of necessity creates grounds for the reinterpretation of laws.[24] Luban accurately notes that the "self-conscious aim of torture is to turn its victim into someone who is isolated, overwhelmed, terrorized, and humiliated . . . to strip away from its victims all the qualities of human dignity."[25]

There are two other elements of torture, pain, and the cruelty of humiliation that we should examine. Elaine Scarry has made the point that "in serious pain the claims of the body utterly nullify the claims of the world."[26] In the context of torture and interrogation, the purported purpose of pain is to break the individual. The purpose is to make the body unable to resist. Thus it is not an accident that the various memoranda written by members of the Bush administration justifying torture often did so under the rubric of counter-resistance techniques. We should note that in perhaps one of the most bizarre examples of how some members of the Bush administration viewed torture, the former secretary of defense issued handwritten approval for what were called aggressive techniques of counter-resistance. In his approval of the proposed aggressive techniques, Donald Rumsfeld wrote, "However, I stand for 8–10 hours a day. Why is standing limited to 4 hours?"[27]

Foucault observes that the decline of the public spectacle of execution in Europe coincided with the formal disappearance of torture, thus making "punishment . . . the most hidden part of the penal process."[28] The removal of torture from the public realm created a whole set of new technologies of punishment. Foucault writes, "Physical pain, the pain of the body itself, is no longer the constituent element of penalty. From being the art of unbearable sensations, punishment has become an economy of suspended rights."[29] Even though punishment has been separated from physical pain, I want to suggest that the practices of punishment as torture haunt us today. It may be important to think about torture not as a practice that occurs during interrogation but as a form of punishment of a body that has been excluded from the mainstream.[30] This means that in the so-called war on terror, the victims of torture were punished both for who they were and for what the torturers perceived that they had done. To practice torture, a set of discursive procedures has to be followed, since subjecting bodies to pain requires that they be excluded from the norm. A series of arguments promulgated by the Bush administration was central to the creation of the conditions for torture in the contemporary empire of liberty. At the core of these arguments were the conceptions that Afghanistan was a failed state and that members of the Taliban militia or those associated with it did not have to be accorded the rights of the Geneva conventions. The words of the memorandum on this matter make clear the reason why this was not considered necessary. The memorandum declares that a failed state constituted a "condition of statelessness and therefore was not a High Contracting Party to the Geneva Conventions for at least that period of time."[31]

The point I wish to make here is that circumstances of torture, like those of death and genocidal violence, require the creation of a set of discursive premises rooted in hierarchical systems of human classification. These grounds have a history and a set of practices that we need to remember; otherwise we see torture and forms of violence as aberrations rather than as possible outcomes of historical logics that may haunt a society. For example, when we grapple with torture in American democracy, it is important that we reflect on the judgment of Chief Justice Roger Taney of the U.S. Supreme Court in the *Dred Scott* case, in which he declared blacks as "having no rights that whites were bound to respect." In a very important sense, the historical wound of racial slavery continues to be central to the constitution of questions of punishment and torture in American democracy.

In his introduction to Colin Dayan's book titled *The Story of Cruel and Unusual*, Jeremy Waldron noted that "when we abolished slavery, we did not abolish it unconditionally, but with the Thirteenth Amendment qualification that slavery is okay for prisoners."[32] In her book, Dayan successfully argues that the "ghost of slavery still haunts our legal language and holds the prison system in thrall."[33] What is interesting is that much of the current debate about torture ignores this ghost.[34]

One of the themes running through these lectures is colonial power. I have attempted to suggest that we cannot think adequately about modernity unless we understand that there was an intimate relationship between coloniality and modernity. So intimate was this relationship that I, together with others, have spoken about a historical process that may properly be called "colonial modernity." From this perspective, I want to close my discussion of torture by reflecting briefly on the Algerian War of Independence.

The controversies over the meaning of one of the fiercest armed struggles for national liberation continue to swirl in our contemporary politics. After the tragedy of 9/11 and the discussions about mounting a war on terror, Gillo Pontecorvo's remarkable film *The Battle of Algiers* became required viewing at the Pentagon. What we are less aware of on this side of the Atlantic is that in February 2005, the French government proposed a law under which French school curricula would be required to depict French colonialism in a positive light. At the same time, the French state rehabilitated members of the Organization de l'Armee Secrete, some of whom had been convicted for crimes during the Algerian War of Independence. My point here is that, in many ways, the event of the Algerian War is a marker within the twentieth century. It is a marker that will not be fully settled until questions about colonial power and its relationship to torture are settled in some fashion.

In the nineteenth century, Algeria was invaded by France, and by the 1870s it was a French colony. In the 1950s, the Algerians launched a war against French colonial occupation. In May 1958, French paratroopers surrounded the Casbah with the objective of breaking a widely supported strike and destroying, where possible, the internal leadership of the National Liberation Front (FLN). The key French general in charge was Jacques Massu. It is now widely acknowledged that in this war torture was a common practice. In a remarkable work on torture practices during the war, Marnia Lazreg writes, "Nevertheless, the professionalization of torture conveyed the message of its acceptance as a war weapon on par with training and shooting. . . . torture was thus pulled out of the shadowy semantic domain in which it lived, and thrust into the forefront of everyday life. . . . it reached deep into the military body."[35]

All the discursive procedures were put in place as the Algerian body was punished. It has been recognized that torture did not yield massive intelligence information during this war. Lazreg observes that "the systematic use of torture during the Algerian War did not help to win the war. . . . The Algerian case reveals that the democratic state is in constant danger of allowing its pre-democratic core to emerge and engage in violations of laws."[36] In the American case, and, I would argue, in the French case as well, there is no return to any predemocratic status of what constitutes an imperial state. An imperial state functions through many repertoires but is not a democratic state unless democracy is narrowly defined as political equality for those populations that belong to the mother country. We therefore need to see torture as one form of violence that is practiced and deployed by power, not as an aberration, but as one of power's possible logics. In many ways, I have been arguing for us to understand these moments and practices as both contingent and historically shaped.

I now come to the third segment of this lecture. I hope to make some points about violence and power by presenting the results of an ethnographic study on the practices of violence in the postcolony of Jamaica. If, in the first two segments of this lecture, I focused on violence that is sponsored and instigated by the state, I now examine violence that is enacted by a group loosely called the urban poor. This shift in focus is necessary in part because my preoccupation with subjectivities requires thinking about agency as a material practice. Here I am always reminded that Friedrich Nietzsche once remarked, "the doing is everything." In thinking about this shift, it has become clear to me that violence enacted by non-state actors can become, as Allen Feldman observes, "a self-legitmating sphere of social discourse and transaction points."[37] What I think is important within this sphere is the way in which the social ontological question about life is posed. So now let us turn to the Caribbean.

Violence in the Jamaican Postcolony

Violence is perhaps the single most discussed and vexing issue in many Caribbean societies today. The number of individuals killed in Jamaica and St. Lucia, the bomb attacks in Trinidad, and the growing number of persons violently killed in Guyana speak not of a mundane crisis in the Caribbean postcolony but of a crisis we have yet to name. This is not a crisis of hegemony or the end of the Bandung project, nor can it be understood, as I suggested a few years ago, as one of "language, life and labor."[38] Crisis as phenomenon morphs and, if not resolved, takes on a life of its own, reproducing itself in different forms. In such contexts, one element of a conjunctural crisis can become a long-term feature of a society, shifting some of the central grounds and practices through which a human community reproduces itself and its ways of life over time. When reflecting on violence in Jamaica and its relationship to power, I am working through power's capillary forms of existence, as a force field that exists in ways other than its conventional state forms. As I review these forms, I suggest, following Foucault, that power is a productive force. Thus, within the urban Jamaican space that I will describe, power operates productively, creating geographical spaces of violence and death while remapping sovereignty.[39]

The construction of these geographical spaces not only sustains subjectivities but does many other things, only two of which I will mention. First, it forces us once again to rethink the relationship between violence and power. Second, it forces us to think about the complexities of subaltern counterhegemonic practices, the genealogy of those practices, and their capacity to change.

Power, Coercion, and Hegemony:
From Racial Slavery to Tutelage (The Jamaican Case)

It is neither the intention nor the purpose of this lecture to engage in an extensive unraveling of the history of nineteenth-century Jamaica. However, because my arguments about the relationship of power to violence suggest a series of shifts in how Jamaican society is conventionally studied, so it is important to review a few critical elements in the historical construction of power in Jamaican society.

The abolition of racial slavery in colonial Jamaica was a watershed for the forms of rule deployed by British colonial power. Racial slavery under British colonialism combined four kinds of violence. Achille Mbembe has observed that colonial sovereignty "rested on three sorts of violence . . . the founding violence . . . [the violence of] legitimation . . . [and] the third form of violence . . . falling well short of . . . 'war,' [recurring] again and again in the most banal and ordinary situations."[40] However, in those instances in which racial slavery was combined with colonial power, power also rested on a fourth leg of violence. If colonial power conventionally ruled through projects of civilization, violent conquest, tutelage, or assimilation, racial slavery required a kind of absolute domination in which the body of the slave was not only property but a thing, a *res* that was outside the social and political mechanisms of the community. The slave existed in what Orlando Patterson has called a state of "social death." However, as I have stated before, the slave's human life was reduced. This reduction was not "bare life" but rather life made superfluous.[41] All this we have rehearsed before, so W. E. B. DuBois's succinct formulation in *Black Reconstruction* that Atlantic slavery represented a form of domination that rested on the "submergence below the arbitrary will of any sort of individual" continues to serve us well.[42]

As a form of domination, the system of racial slavery deployed technologies of rule that targeted the slave body. The objective of this kind of power was not to turn human beings into subjects but into objects and things. In this context, violence was deployed to break and destroy, to remove possibilities and to act immediately upon the person through the body.

The abolition of racial slavery shifted this mode of power in the colonial Caribbean, changing its terrain from a singular focus on the body to an art of creating subjects. But we should not be too sanguine about this shift because, as Diana Paton has pointed out, the shift did not mean the end of certain kinds of punishment. Flogging was reintroduced in the 1850s, and the treadmill became a common feature of plantation life in the postemancipation Caribbean.[43]

There were two principal technologies of colonial rule in Jamaica's postemancipation period, besides colonial violence. The first was Christianity (hence the extensive deployment of Christian missionaries during the period), and the second was the vigorous attempt to turn the ex-slave into a wage laborer. Combined, these two forms of rule sought to create a moral culture that was modeled in part on an imaginary Victorian male respectability, what Horace Russell has called so felicitously the "Christian Black."[44] The creation of this subject provided the ground for power to act outside of naked violence. Power became, in the words of Michel Foucault, a condition for the "management of possibilities."[45] It is of course now well documented that the ex-slaves captured the Christianity of the missionaries and produced a number of Afro-Christian religious practices.[46] The emergence of the religious practices of Myalism and Zionism, what the late Phillip Curtin described as the Africanization of the 1861 Christian Revival, was a process in which Afro-Jamaican subaltern subjects staked out a new ground for fashioning their own humanness. Central to this was the emergence of what Diane Austin-Broos has called a *logic of affliction*. Writing about revivalism, she observes that it was:

> not simply a "mixing" of elements but rather a redefinition of the form of Christianity that the missionaries had brought to Jamaica. . . . [it] was not simply a nativistic movement . . . it was rather a complex of rite and belief that sought to sustain the *logic of affliction* by assimilating elements of Christianity to it[47] (emphasis mine).

Two things about this logic of affliction are critical. Over time this logic became an integral part of a series of narratives about the meanings of black suffering in the New World. These meanings were eventually bolstered by a reinterpretation of the biblical story of the Exodus.[48] Second, the logic of affliction reemerged in various periods in the political language of the Jamaican subaltern as "sufferers" (noun). At this point we are running ahead of our story, but we should note that one of the main features of the present is the erosion and aggressive rejection of this logic by many young males. Indeed I would argue that currently the logic of affliction has been superseded by a different understanding of the Afro-Jamaican subaltern self.

The strivings of Creole nationalism culminated in the island's political and constitutional independence in 1962. However, it is critical to observe that, at the level of the Afro-Jamaican subaltern, while Creole nationalism consolidated itself into a national, state form and proclaimed national sovereignty, the politico-religious doctrines and practices of Rastafari offered an alternative. Rastafari emerged from three sources: an international, diasporic, black religious tradition; a series of contestations between elements of revivalism and early black religious doctrines that reread the Bible in order to discover the causes and meanings of black suffering in the New World; and, finally, growing gender conflict between Afro-Jamaican male subalterns and females who joined in Pentecostalism and revivalism.[49] This latter group was located socially as exploited domestic workers in middle-class homes.[50] Rastafari was to play an important role in the radicalization of the Jamaican political moment in the 1960s. Indeed it was the central force behind the cultural forms that made powerful attempts to refashion popular culture. But Rastafari was not the only source of subaltern rebellion, because alongside it emerged the figure of the *Rude Bwoy*.

The Rudie

Garth White, in his seminal essay on this figure, observes that the "Rude Bwoy is that person, native, who is totally disenchanted with the ruling system; who generally descended from the 'African' in the lower class and who is now armed with ratchets, other cutting instruments and with increasing frequency nowadays, with guns and explosives."[51] Perry Henzell's film *The Harder They Come* provides us with a visual representation of this figure. The film puts together the two male subaltern exemplars of early postcolonial resistance in Jamaica, Rastafari in the figure of Ras Daniel Heartman and Ivan in the figure of Jimmy Cliff. Both are rebellious, but the terms of their rebellion are different.[52] For Ivan, rebellion is captured in the song "You Can Get It If You Really Want," while for the Rastafari, rebellion is captured by the stoicism of the plaintive song "Many Rivers to Cross."

It is accurate to point out that violence was part of the repertoire of rebellion of the Rude Bwoy. However, I want to suggest that this was not just the internalized violence of Fanon, nor the violence of the lumpen proletariat preying upon itself and its community, but rather violence as a strategic instrument that was deployed as an end. In *The Wretched of the Earth*, Fanon notes that violence is a force that makes the native "fearless and restores self-respect."[53] For the Rude Bwoy violence was often a means of creating and safeguarding zones of black masculinity that were at odds with the hegemonic conceptions of the Jamaican nation-state. It was deployed to construct what the Caribbean intellectual George Beckford calls "a mode of life."[54] It marked out a different set of normative terms for this subaltern group's self-conception and in particular emphasized the notion of respect. I want to suggest that what was happening was the following: postcolonial Jamaican society was embedded within a hegemonic framework in which the black majority was viewed as outside, as the great unwashed who could not be trained or civilized. In a profound sense the class, color, and racial schema of Jamaican society located the urban and rural black underclass as unworthy. This was both an epistemological problem of framing and a problem of social ontology. Or to put the case in clear Jamaican nation-language, and in the words of the musician Peter Tosh, the Jamaican social system was a "shits-tem." Inside that framework, dignity and respect were human qualities that male subaltern figures attempted to carve out for themselves. This was the overarching desire of the Rude Bwoy, a self-fashioning that would command respect and dignity on his own terms. But we know that all material practices are fluid. Over time the phenomenon of the Rude Bwoy developed into gangs, and many of them became attached to the Jamaican two-party political system. But there was no easy slide from rebellion to accommodation, incorporation, and eventual transformation into something else. When they were first courted by the political parties, many Rude Bwoys expressed ideas that drew from Rastafari doctrine and, in some instances, the Cuban Revolution. For example, the posters and iconography that decorated many of the small shack dwellings of members of this group ranged from pictures of Haile Selassie (the human-God figure in Rastafari doctrine), Che Guevara, Fidel Castro, and icons of the American Black Power movement to the Communist hammer and

sickle. When they became integrated into the two-party system, many
initially saw themselves as warriors or soldiers. Integration into the
two-party system was accomplished at two levels. First they became
a protective force for communities that waged political war against
each other. Second they became over time the central figures responsible for the distribution of various forms of public works, thereby
embedding themselves firmly within the practices of political clientage. When this process had been consolidated, their transformation
from rebellious figures into *political enforcers* was complete.

In general, therefore, it is safe to say that eventually the Rude
Bwoy was transformed into a political-party warrior. It is at this
point that we should turn to the understanding of political violence
in some urban communities.

War, Violence, and Party Politics

In his 1977 study of violence and politics in Jamaican society,
Terry Lacy argues that one of the critical issues facing that society
in the 1960s and early 1970s was an "internal security situation."
He poses this dilemma as central to the prospects for political change.
Lacy documents how the new ruling elite of Jamaica denounced
"the general attitude of lawlessness; maintained armed vigil; called
for flogging in schools."[55] He then suggests that the group that he
identifies as the lumpen proletariat was responsible for violence and
that its activities created disquiet on the part of the new ruling elite.
He notes:

> This was what the national bourgeoisie called a "criminal" or "hoo-
> ligan" element. Trench Town, Denham Town, Back O'Wall, Moon-
> light City—these names of parts of Western Kingston conveyed im-
> ages of youth gangs, political gangs, Rastafarians, of Prince Henry's
> gang, The Max gang, the Blue Mafia, The Dunkirk gang, . . . the
> Vikings or the Roughest and the Toughest.[56]

Lacy ends his argument on violence by stating that the "lumpen—
proletariat were the primary source of violence *against* the whole

political system whereas over the decade other social classes were the primary source *within* the system"[57] (emphasis in original). There is not enough time in this lecture to engage in arguments about the ambiguous radical or revolutionary agency of the so-called lumpen proletariat or the power of this designation for the urban Jamaican poor in a postcolonial economy. Instead I want to focus on violence from a different angle: not violence as an incipient force of insurgency but rather violence as a way of constructing rule in local communities and as a form of disorder deployed to produce and create order in a localized community space.

There is no longer any dispute in Jamaican political discourse over the historic links between the Jamaican two-party political system and the emergence of political war and a politics of violence. The current debate instead concerns the degree of continuing connection. One question has perplexed many commentators and radical activists. How was it possible for urban and rural oppressed groups to be so divided that they ended up engaging in violence against each other? Why was class solidarity so lacking and seemingly impossible to construct? There are many possible answers to this, but one lies in the two-party political system's construction of the practice of mainstream politics. In this practice, not only was clientage a "mechanism by which to institutionalize a power structure" alongside a politics of scarce benefits, but the Jamaican political party system was also able to construct and maintain a politics of difference based upon one of the oldest political stratagems, the division of friends from enemies.[58]

When developing his conception of the political, the conservative German legal and political theorist Carl Schmitt draws on Machiavellian notions of the political order and argues that "the specific political distinction to which political actions and motives can be reduced is that between friend and enemy."[59] Schmitt continues, "the political enemy need not be morally evil nor aesthetically ugly. . . . But he is nevertheless, the other, the stranger; and it is sufficient for his nature that he is, in a special intense way, existentially something different and alien."[60] The enactment of a form of politics based on a dichotomy between friend and foe that organizes itself into difference is required in contexts in which violence is a necessary feature of political life. Especially intriguing in the Jamaican case was the ability of the two-party system to construct the difference between friend and foe in small, localized, geographical spaces. It is critical to note that these constructions were consistently reinforced by notions of belonging and were enacted through the political dramaturgy of songs, colors, party conferences, dances, popular music, and appropriations of the religious symbolism of both Rastafari and other Afro-Jamaican religious practices. For many who engaged in Jamaican political wars, their political rationale was primarily based on the politics of friend and foe. I now wish to illustrate this empirically by reporting briefly on a series of research findings. I take this tack because any study of violence requires a specific and concrete understanding of the ways in which those who have perpetuated violence and those who have been affected by violence understand it.

The Findings

In a small urban community that we will call Cascade Gardens, extensive ethnographic work was done with individuals who engaged in warfare and those who supported such warfare. One participant called Nigel (not his real name) summed up how violence and political war were viewed. He said:

> The rationale behind it is that if we kill off one set then there won't be any votes. . . . Individuals growing up learned that the person who were [sic] fighting against you and you were fire shot at were *our enemy*. So if they saw us anywhere and hear where we stay they will kill us[61] (emphasis mine).

Another person pointed out that the enemy (who lived a few blocks away) would behave similarly. Thomas (not his real name) stated that "Anybody who dem catch . . . Have to dead. You naw mek you enemy live. At that time I shared the same sentiment."[62] In these contexts differences were rearticulated as reasons and ratio-nales for war. Nobody admitted to fighting for a job, a house, or any scarce resource or benefit that was normally distributed by the Jamaican political system through clientage. Instead, people spoke about party, community, defense of self, and being a warrior. According to one person, "from you hear stone a lick pon you fence you know say you have fi bleach. A de same youth wah you cook with and you know and ting. So you go pon the corner."[63] The construction of difference that was organized around practices of friend and foe, along with the reinscribing of this difference through rituals of belonging, meant, in the words of one community resident, "We now become instead of natural African people, laborities and PNP."[64]

There were, or are, two forms of violence in the Jamaican context. One was, or is, *political violence*, which reached its peak in the 1980 general election when over eight hundred persons died in an electoral contest fought like a civil war. The Jamaican poet Lorna Goodison has memorialized this event in the poem "Jamaica 1980." She writes:

For over all this edenism
hangs the smell of necromancy
and each man eats his brother's flesh
. . . We've sacrificed babies
and burnt mothers[65]

Goodison's poem captures the ways in which the so-called island paradise, the place of the sweet smells of plants and secret streams, becomes a place of death. In this land of death, differences constructed within subaltern groups now play out on a field of war. This is not genocide but death deployed as terror, as a tactic to de-stabilize the conventional field of electoral politics. I would argue that, nearly thirty years after this event, the tactics deployed in this political war repeat themselves in enactments of violence in Jamaica. I would also argue that the Jamaican political process has not had a full and open discussion of this traumatic event, and this in part allows the event and its reverberations to linger on as a loud silence in the island's contemporary history.

The second form of violence to which I wish to draw our attention was, or is, a violence that links itself to the operation of power in small geographical spaces (lanes, streets, small communities divided into zones). Political violence and what I call *intimate violence*, or violence enacted in small spaces and conducted upon known bodies, are sometimes linked. But they must be understood differently. I would argue that the practices of political violence engender the other form of violence. I now turn to a discussion of violence and its relationship to power and death within the specific conditions of the Jamaican postcolony.

Violence, Death, and the Making of Duppies

Violence, as I have indicated before, is both a difficult and a slippery subject. Its primary enactment in terms of physicality and the infliction of pain involves assaults on personhood. As a practice violence is about spectacle. To be effective as order, it must first awe and then create fear. Even though violence kills or maims, sometimes its logic is not about death per se but about its deployment in the production of order. Genocidal violence seeks to cleanse and purify to create an order of purity. Torture aims to exclude and mark bodies, to further punish the excluded and mark difference. The violence in the Jamaican postcolony is also about order, but a specific kind of order. It is an order in which those already excluded perpetuate violence as representative enactments of their lives, which are already marginal in a society that marks them as not worthy. In other words, it is in part an enactment of lives that are not grievable.

We noted earlier in this lecture that Hannah Arendt suggests that violence is "ruled by the means-end category."[66] Hopefully we have demonstrated that this framework for thinking about violence is inadequate. If, for a moment, we agree with Foucault about power and see it as capacity, as the designation of a relationship, rooted in a network of the social,[67] then violence is not a means-end instrument but one aspect of power. In other words, violence is not just a technology of power or a premodern instrument that is negated through the creation of a disciplinary, liberal society. How does violence in Jamaican society illustrate this, and what is violence's relationship to death in Jamaican society? At this point in the lecture, we must confront the issue of sovereignty.

Achille Mbembe has suggested that the expression of "sovereignty resides, to a large degree, in the power and the capacity to dictate who may live and who must die."[68] Here of course Mbembe is pointing us to one of the chief features of sovereignty—its finality. In much of political philosophy, we have become accustomed to speaking of sovereignty as a form of rule, a power that is the final arbitral agent, independent of external influences. We should remember that the demand for sovereignty was also the great political call of the anticolonial movement and of subsequent demands for other forms of decolonialization. I wish, however, to complicate this conventional understanding of national sovereignty by shifting away from our rightly fierce claims for national and cultural sovereignties to suggest a meaning in which different forms of self-fashioning are critical to forms of rule. In other words, I want to remove sovereignty from the domain of rule constructed around the making of the nation-state and bring it to the ground of the local. By moving in this direction, I am suggesting that in those nation-states where hegemony has been broken we need to understand violence at the micro level.

As I make this shift, I want to suggest that sovereignty need not be a large-scale, national operation. In addition, since notions of belonging are integral to practices of rule, in many circumstances the enactment of belonging also operates at a micro level. Therefore I suggest that in many urban Jamaican communities there has been a shift in the grounds of belonging as the legitimacy of the postcolonial state has been eroded. One resident of Cascade Gardens put it well.

> There was no money, there was no food, there was no hope. Politi-
> cians had failed. They don't see nobody to look up to, because as far
> as it go dem no cater for nobody. . . . everything drop, every man fe
> himself, everybody fe dem food. So everybody pon dem own.[69]

It is within this space that other figures emerge: the area leader and,
eventually, the *Shotta Don.*

In the early Jamaican postcolony, active subaltern currents operated in opposition to the hegemony and sovereign power of a native
elite. These forces did not engage in huge rebellions but practiced a
form of cultural guerrilla warfare, seeking to challenge the norms of
citizenship and its values in what the late Rex Nettleford has called
the "battle for space."[70] In this situation the Jamaican Creole nation-
state did not fully establish its hegemony.[71] A consequence of this
failure was the state's inability to establish hegemonic notions of
citizenship to which all classes and social groups could adhere. This
in turn meant that, instead of a narrative of citizenship with its
rituals of belonging practiced through different performances, these
rituals of belonging and solidarity were practiced through community linkages inside politically controlled parameters. These practices were shaped by a social context of deep class and color divi-
sions and by a discourse that emphasized "outside" and "inside,"
with the urban poor continually positioned as "dem de people down
there." In the present situation, belonging occupies and works
through micro spaces within communities. Within some of these
micro spaces, the area leader and then the Shotta Don rules.

The Shotta Don: A Figure of Death

There are many features of the area leader who then becomes the
Shotta Don, but two are critical for our current discussion.[72] The
first is that many area leaders mixed Rastafari symbols with black
nationalism. The typical operational base of the area leader is organized around an economic venture such as a small shop. At many
of these bases (they are called bases in popular discourse), murals

of Marcus Garvey, Bob Marley, and Malcolm X adorn the walls. Dances are frequently held at these locations. When the dances are held, persons from neighboring, opposing, and sometimes hostile political communities are often welcomed. The second feature of note is that the rule of the area leader functions through a set of community codes enforced primarily by male individuals. In this context violence operates in two ways. In the first the enforcement of the code itself can be violent.[73] Second, once "war" breaks out between communities, warriors take up their guns and engage in firefights, often to the death. So how does death function in these operations?

One striking feature of young men who engage in violence is their conversations with each other, in which they often ask each other, "how many duppies you mek?"[74] If, as Bataille argues, death is a form of destruction and a sacrifice that is irreversible, as well as a spectacle that haunts life itself, then for many males involved in violence death is a spectacle that affirms their lives. This is particularly so because in the middle of war or violence other life-affirming activities are uncommon. Listen to the voice of another resident of Cascade Gardens:

> Yu have time when every Sunday, every Saturday, you have funeral inside ya. For years you don't have a wedding, because it is like a trend. This week Tom going bury, next week is John, so we making preparation for that funeral. People just dead, and some of we just take it like joke, and we dress up and go a de funeral. The funeral is like a fashion show. And the latest fashion go a funeral when somebody ask you a who dead, you ask: A who?[75]

In such communities, young males expect death as an affirmation that they have lived, and the burial ritual is marked not only by fashion but by gun salutes at the graveside. However, it should be noted that this is not the general view of the community, even of those engaged in violence. As one young man called Marcus (not his real name) puts it, as he became more involved, he had "no feelings at all" and "had to turn to God to seek answer due to vibes and tension." It seems, therefore, that any radical transformation of Jamaica has to begin with the recognition that not only has Creole state hegemony collapsed but a new form of politics has arisen, in which organized communities operate outside the constitutional and juridical norms of the nation-state. This is not a situation of dual power as a prelude to revolution, because the radical subaltern self-fashioning that extensively drew on Rastafari and a politics of radical black nationalism has also collapsed. This collapse within subaltern geographical spaces means that the area leader is rapidly losing his dominance and is being replaced by the Shotta Don.

From Rude Bwoy to Shotta Don

In a song titled "Petty Thief," which is also a remarkable commentary on urban Jamaican life, the dance hall DJ Bounti Killa observes that the petty thief is a predatory figure within the urban community and not a Rude Bwoy. The song notes the complete transformation of a postcolonial rebel figure (the Rude Bwoy) into a commanding *figure of vengeance* (the Shotta Don). This figure of vengeance both seeks to destroy and searches for ways to enter the mainstream of society. Two episodes were central to the formation of this figure of the Shotta Don, and ironically they both had to do with the failure of peace processes among urban subaltern groups. One of these peace processes was attempted in the 1970s, and the other in 1999.

In the aftermath of what is now called the Green Bay massacre of 1978, political enforcers from both political parties organized a peace treaty. The ambush killing of political enforcers by the Jamaican military shook many enforcers' political ties. The two major figures in the peace effort were Claude Massop from Tivoli Gardens, the main Jamaica Labour Party (JLP) stronghold at the western end of Kingston, and Aston "Buckie" Thompson from the People's National Party (PNP). The peace treaty was warmly welcomed by many of the political enforcers and had the backing of prominent individuals, in particular Bob Marley. The peace process was organized and managed by a council that met regularly at the Ambassador Theatre in West Kingston. Its advocates demanded a program of public works for the unemployed male youths of urban Kingston. In an outspoken speech at one of the rallies held in support of the treaty, Buckie Thompson declared: "After peace now, we want to see improvement in living conditions. We want work in general and government must put more in youth programs." Echoing this call, another individual stated, "Unity wonderful but we want better housing, better living standard for all people whether JLP or PNP. We cannot allow politicians to come into West Kingston and divide the youths anymore. The situation must remedy."[76] Individuals close to the process have pointed out that many of the discussions at the Ambassador Theatre centered on the possibility of a new political party of Rastafari to be funded with Marley's money. This peace process did not last and was buried with the killing of Massop in Jamaica and Thompson in New York.

Some individuals who attended the various peace council meetings recalled in interviews with me both the promise of the treaty and its example. Twenty-one years later, in 1999, some of these figures made a second attempt. However, if the first peace treaty was driven by a desire for unity in the face of certain death at the hands of state forces, the second one was driven by two elements: the economic activities of individuals who had used their positions as political enforcers to garner state resources and a growing feeling in many urban communities that violence had taken its toll.

The second peace process was not as centralized as the first. There was no central advisory council, although various attempts were made to pull the leadership of communities together into a combined peace movement. However, it was clear that in the twenty-one years since the collapse of the first peace movement, many urban communities had become balkanized. Wherever peace was declared because of the exhaustion of a community, criminal activity declined. These activities included rape and petty theft.[77] In community spaces where peace was enacted, forums of community justice emerged. These forums were sometimes organized to include individuals within the communities who were seen as elders or who enjoyed some amount of respect. Elements of black nationalist ideas and Rastafari were again used to undergird declarations of unity and peace.

In one community, the peace process encouraged classes in radical black history and the development of a literacy program. However, in all the communities peace was unstable. Peter Tosh had declared at the peace concert in 1978 that there would be no peace without justice. The second effort at peace collapsed for two reasons. The first was the inability of the peacemakers to provide economic development in communities. The second was the emergence of a generation of young males called *Shottas*, who did not buy into either of the two main ideologies of radical subaltern Afro-Jamaica, Rastafari or radical black nationalism. These Shottas challenged many area leaders, became leaders themselves, and engaged in predatory activities. The emergence of this avenging figure is the main sign of the crisis. The figure of the Shotta Don does not seek to explain and understand his social location by reference to any logic of black suffering. For this figure, the Jamaican postcolony is itself a predatory state, and the ways of contesting it that are rooted in subaltern rebellious cultures have all failed. There is only one way out, to obtain enough capital through extortion, government contracts, and haulage business to influence the formal, two-party system.

The Shotta Don as an avenging figure establishes rule in communities by the force of death. In such circumstances, death is not a rupture but a norm to be deployed. Violence becomes the foreclosure of possibilities and is arbitrary. In those contexts, local rule is about the absolute power of death. Also, violence must now be brutal in a special sense, and, significantly, rape becomes a regular feature of violent attacks.

What are we to make of this figure of the Shotta Don and his reconfiguration of violence and power? There are many similarities in the ways in which death and pain are deployed in all three circumstances that I have described. But there are vast differences with regard to violence as purification. If genocide enacts a death-drive of purification and torture enacts violence as punishment then, for the Jamaican, Shotta Don violence creates fear primarily in order to rule. In all of these cases, violence either becomes power or is enacted as power. In each case, the human is negated. In a recent essay, Judith Butler asks about the establishment of the familiar "as the criterion by which a human life is grievable."[78] It seems to me that, both inside the empire of liberty and in some sites of the postcolonial world, we are faced with this question of the human. This is not the question, who are we? Instead the question is, what are we? Or to put this another way, what makes us human? The question is forcefully brought home to us by the various enactments of violence as power. In such a context death becomes, not a boundary, as Aristotle once said, but the very horizon of life. And security, not freedom, shapes how we live. Is this what we want?

[4]

THE END OF HISTORY OR THE INVENTION OF EXISTENCE

Critical Thought and Thinking about the Human

The real leap consists in introducing invention into existence.   —FRANTZ FANON

One cannot "unsettle" the coloniality of power without a redescription of the human outside of the terms of our own present descriptive statement of the human.

—SYLVIA WYNTER

Crim, you can take it from me. If I ever give you freedom, Crim, then all your future is mine, 'cause whatever you do in freedom name is what I make happen.

—GEORGE LAMMING

I BEGIN THIS final lecture by expressing my deep appreciation to all of you who have attended this lecture series. Your engaging comments and questions have been important, making it more like a conversation than a formal lecture series. You may recall that I began this lecture series, or conversation, by stating that I was trying to do three things. First, I was not working through any theory of power but rather was attempting to think about our current moment. Reformulating the meaning of the phrase *empire of liberty*, I posited a possible language in which we might think about the relationship between power, domination, and the questions of freedom and desire today. Second, I suggested that the current description of our present condition, particularly in regard to America, as a "state of exception" generated by the policies of the Bush Administration, is ahistorical. Third, I was making an attempt to shift some of the categories we commonly deploy. With reference to the ahistorical character of the "state of exception" and American power, I suggested the following: if we use "state of exception" to describe the current moment of domestic American power, we miss the historical "sites of exception," racial slavery and dependent Native American nations, which have always been constituted by American power. As a consequence, I have argued that within the United States the systems of racial slavery and the conquest of the indigenous population meant that laws in these communities were never about rights but were always about death, torture, and pain. This is not an original point, and it emerges from my understanding of the labors of the radical black intellectual tradition and its various writers and thinkers, particularly W. E. B. DuBois.

But I also find it interesting that Walter Benjamin, in his "Theses on the Philosophy of History," makes a similar point when discussing the idea of "states of emergency." In his discussion, Benjamin makes the compelling case that "the tradition of the oppressed teaches us that the 'state of emergency' in which we live is not the exception but the rule. We must attain to a conception of history that is in keeping with this insight."[1] This is an important point to which I will return. I will suggest that one of the major problems of critical thought today is that it does not focus on the traditions of the oppressed as they relate to thought.

In my second lecture, I posited the idea that, when thinking about questions of race and democracy, it may be useful to rethink the idea that democracy is an incomplete project to be completed by a series of prefixes, whether radical, direct, or participatory. Rather, we should see democracy as an empty signifier and a horizon always described by its lack. I argued that democracy was formulated in Western thought in response to a series of questions about the construction of political rule and, to paraphrase Maurice Godelier, was born out of the basic political relations in Greece between "citizens and noncitizens, free men and slaves." In such a context, democracy could be theorized, but the conflict between freemen and slaves was invisible and thus not theorized.

Of course, while Solon's reforms led to the abolition of debt bondage, they did not abolish slavery. After the reforms, slaves in Greek society were imported and as foreigners were called barbarians. These slaves were outside the polity, while democracy was within the polis, so that one dimension of Greek freedom was the freedom to enslave the barbarian. That freedom belonged to the freeborn Greek male, whether he was an aristocrat or commoner. Greek freedom allowed the enslavement of another. It was a freedom predicated upon enslavement. It was the kind of freedom that was practiced during the period of racial slavery in America. In Greek society the slave was reduced to the state of an animate tool. In Aristotle's words, the slave was "a part of the master in the sense of being but a separate part of his body."[2] In such a context, the slave was human chattel, listed as the "first and most indispensable kind of property."[3] Following the arguments of the Caribbean historian Elsa Goveia, I made the point that racial slavery was a system in which the slave was "property in the person." From this perspective, I argued in the second lecture that human groups who experience racial slavery and colonialism in what I have been calling colonial modernity experience historical and social trauma. They experience historical trauma in which social wounds cannot simply be erased by democratic inclusion. Instead, these wounds produce cries, not laments. These cries force upon us another set of questions—about living, about what we are, and about the nature of freedom itself.

I also suggested that when we think of political modernity, we should rethink what we mean. When making this suggestion I posited that the encounter between what has been called the Old World and the New World, which was initiated by the voyages of Columbus beginning in 1492, should be seen as the inaugural event of modernity, indeed, as the *instituting event*.[4] By this I mean that

Columbus's voyages opened a new epoch, changed the relationships between what was thought possible and what was thought impossible, and broke the bounds of then-accepted temporalities, ushering in different configurations and framing new questions for human societies. Acknowledging the Columbian voyages as an instituting event means opening up another set of pathways into the meanings of political modernity and politics, meanings that are central to this lecture series.

My third lecture concerned violence. I engaged with Hannah Arendt, quarreled with her view that the presence of violence evacuates power, and noted that she misses the complex character of power. Contrary to Arendt, I suggested that violence can be power and that in its performance as power violence seeks to trap bodies. As power, violence does not necessarily make death its primary objective, and sometimes death becomes a means to an end. Violence as power is about enforcing discipline and an order based upon frequent enactments of death. Because of violence's intimate relationship to pain and death, we tend to see it as existing outside the boundaries of power. I therefore wish to link violence and power once again. When discussing violence, I shifted from the registers of intellectual history and political theory and reported on an ethnographic study that I conducted on violence in Jamaica. The study focused on an inner city and a group of young men called Shottas. This study led to my own understanding of the ways in which death became a performance of a "negative self-fashioning freedom," a self-fashioning that operates in the direction of negating life.

It has been critical to review the main elements of my previous arguments, since they situate this final lecture. From my first lecture, I have been tracking the ways in which power is constructed, the ways in which we as human beings become subjects. I have also been arguing that we live at a historical juncture that cannot be described in the way that Arendt described parts of the twentieth century, as simply "dark times." I have been arguing that perhaps we live in a moment in which power organizes itself as *free-dom* and in doing so both obscures and directs our intellectual energies so that it is difficult to think in new ways.[5] One of the purposes of these lectures is to suggest possible directions for thinking anew, and it is to this that I now turn.

Habits of Thinking

Let me begin my reflections on thinking anew by first referring to our current habits. Our present habits of thinking linger in part because we have not examined how they were acquired and in part because we often think in historical analogies rather than historically. But there is another reason why many of us have not been able to break our habits of the mind. That reason has to do with what I call *epistemological location*. In the field of critical political theory and thought, a series of events (the American Revolution, the French Revolution, the Commune in Paris, the formation of the Soviets in 1905, the Spanish Civil War of 1936, May 1968, and the Portuguese Revolution of 1974) have become the primary sources and resources of critique. Some of these events continue to stimulate our radical political imagination. This is so much the case that Alan Badiou speaks of the "unconquerable nostalgia of May 1968" while proclaiming in 1988, before the collapse of apartheid in South Africa, that the "Age of Revolution is over." The aforementioned events are important, but they are not the only ones that can be deployed as resources for critical thinking. But I am not talking simply about constructing a broader field of events or correcting epistemic blind spots through fuller representations. Rather, I am pointing to a *way of thinking*, a genealogy of how critical and radical theory runs along certain tracks already constructed for it.

I will make my point concretely. In a book that attempts to work through possible meanings of human emancipation for our times, Alex Callinicos notes that "Eurocentrism is deeply embedded in historical thought."[6] He then confronts the implications of this statement and calls for a decentering of European history and thought as the singular model of human progress. Yet Callinicos is unable to think deeply about the implications of his own judgment. The question before us is not about fuller and more complete representation of human cultures in the domain of thought, specifically critical thought. If this were the primary matter at stake, then only the broadening and diversification of our intellectual resources would be required. So while I agree that there is both an ethical and intellectual necessity for decentering Western thought, something else is required. What is that something? It is this. When we decenter, from what gaze do we decenter? From what angle do we begin to ask questions?

Some time ago, Walter Benjamin observed that thinking "involves not only the flow of thoughts, but their arrest as well."[7] To confront the arrest of thought, we need to decenter and to engage in intellectual pluralism. But we need to ask new questions that emerge from this process of decentering, questions that shift the old ones that we have become acquainted with. To get to these questions, we may have to reorder the categories of thought in which we do social and critical theory. The operation that DuBois successfully achieved in *Black Reconstruction* makes that text relevant today. My argument about habits of thinking concerns how the categories of thought that frame our thinking have become so fixed that even when we decenter we examine with the same eyes. Thus we are not able to see the different questions raised either about freedom or political life, questions that reside, in the words of Sylvia Wynter, between the "interstices of history."[8] For the remainder of this lecture, I will attempt to operate from within those interstices as I see them, while thinking about critical thought. In the end I will point to one possible ground from which we may begin to elaborate a radical politics. In the development of my arguments for this lecture, two figures are important as sources. The first is Georg Wilhelm Friedrich Hegel, and the second is Frantz Fanon.

Hegel and the End of History

I begin with Hegel and the end of history. I do not wish to rehabilitate Hegel (he does not need my assistance for this to happen), but I find it intriguing that in the last decade or so, one of his central ideas has come to frame some currents of hegemonic Western thought. So in terms of some of the issues facing critical thought, we can productively begin by thinking about the end of history.

In his *Lectures on the Philosophy of World History*, Hegel notes that "every state is an end in itself, its internal development and evolution follow a necessary progression whereby the rational, i.e. justice and the consolidation of freedom gradually emerges."[9] For Hegel, "freedom is the one authentic property of the spirit," which is self-consciousness. Thus, when he writes that the work of the spirit is "to produce itself, to make itself its own object, and to gain knowledge of itself in this way to exist for itself," we know that Hegel is thinking about man existing in a search for his essence. For Hegel, such a search is both teleological and theological. In Hegel's view the spirit is a product of itself, and it strives to fulfill its capacity and its desire. Once this striving has been achieved, "the end in the historical process is the freedom of the subject . . . and the end of the world spirit is realized through the freedom of each individual." This is his teleological point. To make his theological point, since "God is omnipresent, he is present in everyone and appears in everyone's consciousness; and this is the world spirit,"[10] the spirit becomes God's wish. Hopefully we do not need to be reminded that for Hegel the history of the world moves from East to West; in his view, Africa has no history. And it is interesting that the notion of the "end of history" emerges with the apparent triumph of Western liberalism at the end of the Cold War.

But before we proceed further, I draw your attention to one aspect of Nietzsche's reading of Hegel. In his *Untimely Meditations*, Nietzsche is critical of the drive for completeness in German philosophy and of the ways in which this drive works by revealing itself to itself. Of course, this is not peculiar to Hegel but pertains to a significant segment of Western thought, in spite of more recent attempts by a set of thinkers to critique totality in what we may call the post-structuralist moment. However, I am presently interested in how this drive in Western thought becomes part of the practices of contemporary power at the level of discourse, and in how, in doing this, it ties itself into a hard, tripartite knot of freedom, man, and God.

Obviously therefore, when I speak of the end of history, I am not referring to Francis Fukuyama's 1993 book *The End Of History and the Last Man*. Rather, I am pointing to the close fit in some strains of dominant contemporary Western thought between questions about the essence of man, history, and God. Let me recall for you President George W. Bush's third State of the Union address: "We go forward with confidence, because this call of history has come to the right country, the liberty we prize is not America's gift to the world, it is God's gift to humanity. . . . we do not claim to know all the ways of Providence, yet we can trust in them, placing our confidence in the loving God behind all of life, and all of history."[11] Some would argue that what we have in this statement is a return to the religious or the theological in dominant and hegemonic thought. But let me ask, when has Western thought been fully free of the theo-political? When have we ever lived in a fully post-religious world? And, by juxtaposition, do we live in a post-secular world? By post-secular I do not necessarily mean an increase in the meaningfulness of religion but rather a changed attitude toward the modern state's own secularist self-understanding. One current, dominant strain of thought holds that *free-dom* becomes the telos, becomes the matrix for the end of human history, and that within such a framework history becomes the working out of a fateful destiny. This is not the telos of a striving toward human perfectibility but rather one of arrival at a destination that unfolds through strife and in which the arrival now signals closure. Jacques Derrida once noted that striving toward perfectibility can be a source of perversion. It seems to me that perversion also happens when there is closure, when the striving becomes absolute, when freedom becomes closed, not open.

How does the idea of the end of history relate to the current conjuncture of globalization, our current modernity, and what I call the empire of liberty? At the level of political economy, we know that globalization creates concentrations of wealth alongside vast exclusion and misery. Within this logic of unequal structures, globalization is *urbi et orbi*, everywhere and anywhere operating as a kind of hyperbolic accumulation that strives not just to homogenize the globe but to be a totality. When discussing globalization, Jean-Luc Nancy observes that "the West has come to encompass the world."[12] Nancy also remarks that when this happens, the West disappears. I would disagree. In his essay "The West and the Rest: Discourse and Power," Stuart Hall notes that the West is an idea, a concept that conjures verbal and visual languages, models of comparison, and criteria of evaluation.[13] So within the framework of globalization, the West does not disappear but consolidates its power. Jean-Luc Nancy states that, as a civilization, the West represented the universal and reason. He then notes that up until now "one cannot say that any other configuration of the world or any other philosophy of the universal and of reason have challenged that course."[14] I do not wish to critique this statement other than to observe that this is an extreme case of epistemological location. Is it not possible that the critical thought of the West is exhausted? In other words, might there exist another possible meaning for the end of history, not the fulfillment of reason, nor that of freedom and self-consciousness, but rather the "end of the history" for the universalism of the West as the *only* generative concept and language for the project of human emancipation? Please note that I am not speaking here of the end of meta-narratives, nor the flexible network of language games that, in Lyotard's view, requires "agonistics as a founding principle" in a so-called postmodern period. Rather, I am speaking about categories of thought embedded within language, categories that blind us so that we cannot see new questions.

In 1951 Hannah Arendt observed that, since the nineteenth century, Western political thought had remained "impenetrably silent and insular in confronting specifically modern questions."[15] I take this one step further to suggest that when colonialism, empire, and racial slavery, as instituting events of modernity, are excluded from the conceptual frameworks of political and critical thought, then that thought becomes what the late Clifford Geertz called "local knowledge."[16]

Ethics and Critical Thought

One current attempt to grapple with this problem in critical political and social thought and criticism is a turn to ethics. In this ethical turn Emmanuel Levinas is an important figure. And rightly so, since his elaboration of *the ethics of the other* in part flows from his grappling with the character of Nazism as a totality and as a system of domination through death and pain. Part of Levinas's critique stems from his understanding that freedom and, as a consequence, human creativity were made impossible by Fascism. Of course, critiques of Fascism remain a touchstone and have generated much critical thought in Western political theory.[17] The point here is that historically catastrophic events generate their own questions. So if a particular set of questions emerged from one set of catastrophic events, what questions emerge from others? Here I am pointing to the relationships of catastrophic events to each other and the traces they leave in our contemporary world. So I am not arguing for a narrow conception of thought of this or that intellectual tradition, nor am I suggesting that traditions operate in isolated silos. Rather, I am positing that the questions posed to us by the inauguration of colonial modernity work to shape our contemporary questions and that we continue to ignore them or do not recognize their centrality. Let me take one example.

At the level of polity, the questions that emerged with Thomas Hobbes in the seventeenth century concerned rule and sovereign power. Hobbes himself notes that he developed his ideas when England was "burning with the questions of the rights of rulers and the duties of subjects, forerunners of an approaching war."[18] In this context he writes, "I authorize and give up my right of governing myself, to this man or assembly of men on the condition, that thou give up thy right to him and authorize all his actions in like manner."[19] From this perspective Hobbes constructs a sovereign power and, in a moment of metaphorical thinking, compares sovereign power to the case of a child's submission to a father. It is crucial to note that, when Hobbes discusses laying aside rights, he says it is done either by renunciation or by transfer. In other words, the individual willingly gives up his or her rights for a common purpose. This was not the situation with colonial conquest. By the seventeenth century, when European colonial empires already held sway, another series of questions was being posed about rule, subjects, and rights. These questions were of a different character than the ones Hobbes formulated and attempted to answer. One episode that illuminates these different questions was the debate between Bartolomé de Las Casas and Juan Ginés de Sepúlveda in 1550. The nub of the debate was the question posed by Sepúlveda: on what basis could the rights of the conquered native populations in the New World be abrogated? The debate between Las Casas and Sepúlveda concerned the basis for the denial of rights, not sovereign rule. The political logics of these two questions move in two different directions. Thus one question that faces us in critical thought is broached by the debate between Las Casas and Sepúlveda: how does the abrogation of rights relate to and shape the conception of rights itself? It is clear that when we ask this question, we are on different grounds of political thought and philosophy. In other words, the issues raised by colonial power about conquest, possession, and the intellectual basis for creating systems of servitude over groups of people are political logics that complicate not only rule and rights but also our responses to them. I am arguing that the discourses and practices that opposed various abrogations offer us insights that we may add to our repertoire of critical thought. Let me give you one final example of what I mean. The eighteenth-century English historian and planter Bryan Edwards, a figure sympathetic to colonial power, observes that for colonial government, "the leading principle on which the government is supported is fear; or a sense of that absolute coercive necessity which leaving no choice of action, *supercedes all questions of rights*"[20] (emphasis mine). The political logics of these sets of practices unfold another set of debates in a different direction.

Rights and Abrogation

At the core of the abrogation of rights, coercion, and wars of conquest was the central question of who and what is a human being. For Western thought this question of the human has been answered in different ways, ranging from man's relationship to the divine, to Cartesian anxieties about the body, to Martin Heidegger's notion of a being that is created out of a void but that is nevertheless connected. However, within the domain of conventional scholarship, we have not spent much time thinking about this question of who and what is a human being from the perspective of human beings who were considered to be non–human beings. This means that our answers about the human typically have a framing, normative perspective that draws from dominant discourse. This allows many of these answers to operate within a philosophical *anthropos* of white or European normativeness. Paul Ricoeur tells us that history is a flux of events and that within that flux the advent of "man" was mediated.[21] Let me twist Ricoeur a bit: the flux of the event (colonial modernity) inaugurated both man and knowledge of man. This knowledge leaves deposits and traces that we have to wrestle with. Today we need to recognize the limits of these deposits and traces. So let me return to the end of history, and suggest that there needs to be another end of history.

It is a conceptual end of history. It is an end of history for reason, not as meta- narrative but as particular categories of thought about the human that presently reside in dominant philosophical anthropology.[22] Perhaps we are at a moment in the history of critical thought in which the labor of the negative is to create anew. For help in this labor, I turn to my second figure, Frantz Fanon.

Fanon and the New

Why Fanon? At the end of John Edgar Wideman's recent novel *Fanon*, the author creates an imaginary political meeting attended by Fanon. Before Fanon speaks to the meeting, Wideman uses the narrator's voice to meditate on maps. Invoking a certain mapping of the world, a mapping that erases others, Wideman as narrator writes, "Fanon understands it, the map that erases him by erasing itself by erasing him, can be flipped over to its unwritten side and then perhaps you could begin a fresh drawing of the world."[23] I think about critical thought from within the interstices of history by working through Fanon because he is, I believe, a twentieth-century figure who has posed some questions about our contemporary world.

A little over a decade ago, Stuart Hall raised a similar question: "Why Fanon?"[24] Making the point that every rereading is ultimately political, Hall suggests that part of the attraction of *Black Skin, White Masks* is its multivocality. He also argues that Fanon misconstrued Lacan, Freud, and Hegel and that these acts of misconstrual produced remarkable insights. On the other hand, Lewis Gordon in his 1995 text *Fanon and the Crisis of European Man* argued that Fanon continues to be relevant in broad terms. Gordon notes, "Fanon embodies a crisis in the very effort to study and forge a better world for human beings. The crisis itself has been articulated as a form of bad faith in which the ability to construct a *tomorrow* is concealed."[25] Both of these positions were part of a debate at the time about Fanon. So what is the politics by which I am offering a rereading of segments of *Black Skin, White Masks*? My preoccupation has been with representation and subjectivity and how they are profoundly shaped by power's drive for total domination. I would argue that the theorist and activist Fanon was supremely concerned with these matters.

By working with Fanon in this way I am neither rehabilitating him as a Caribbean thinker, nor even as a postcolonial figure necessary to the field of postcolonial studies. Instead I want to work with and through some of the questions he posed, because from his location as a colonialized, racialized subject he formulated a series of basic questions that continue to resonate in our present. My argument is not about whether we are beyond Fanon or not, rather it is about thinking through the questions he posed, not the answers he gave. I issue a caveat here. These questions are not perpetual ones existing for all time, but they were posed so sharply in a context of profound global changes at the time that perhaps we have yet to face their enormous implications. At another level, I wish to think with and through Fanon in this lecture because he confronts Hegel and overturns the idea of the other as a permanent fixture of human ways of living. In doing this, I am following the lead of Charles Long, who with reference to Hegel's master–slave dialectic notes that the "hardness of life was not the oppressor; the oppressor was the occasion, for the experience but not the datum of the experience itself."[26]

As I think through Fanon, I offer a rereading of the last two chapters of *Black Skin, White Masks* and the last chapter of *The Wretched of the Earth*. But before we examine these texts, let me say something about Fanon's writing.

For Fanon, writing was about engagement and a form of criticism in which language could be used to shape new categories. Categories are never stable for Fanon; he forms them, deploys them, and then releases them, thereby creating a style of writing in which his own restlessness becomes the operating principle. In Fanon's writing there is improvisation as he confronts reality, shakes it, and then recasts the categories in which we think about a set of specific issues. In Fanon's thought, colonialism and racism are systems of power and linguistic events with different levels of insertion into the world. Consequently his writing is constructed through different registers of the speech-act in which temporalities are often juxtaposed.

In perhaps one of the finest readings of Fanon, Ato Sekyi-Otu observes that "Fanon's discourse was dramaturgical in form."[27] He then adds that Fanon writes in a language of "political experience." Fanon's texts themselves are political acts; they form a narrative of the political while participating in and defining the political. I have spent a moment reflecting on Fanon's writing because it is within the act of writing, which is similar to *the act of making*, that we begin to see another aspect of Fanon's radical political praxis.

The last two chapters of *Black Skin, White Masks* are devoted to two issues, "The Negro and Recognition," and a conclusion that invokes Karl Marx's *The Eighteenth Brumaire of Louis Bonaparte*. Within the chapter "The Negro and Recognition," I want to focus on the segment titled "The Negro and Hegel." Fanon tells us that he turns to Hegel because the "Black man is a former slave," and he wishes to confront this history of slavery and its meanings for the present by juxtaposing one of the core models of the Western master-slave dialectic with racial slavery. For Fanon, Hegel's master-slave dialectic is one in which the drive of the dialectic is an "absolute reciprocity which must be emphasized." He cites Hegel's *Phenomenology of the Mind* and notes that for Hegel both the slave and the master had to recognize "themselves as mutually recognizing each other."[28] In Fanon's reading of Hegel, in order to be oneself, to be human, "the concept of recognition is essential."[29] For the Hegelian master-slave dialectic to operate, both slave and master must desire reciprocal recognition. However, in Fanon's thinking this master-slave dialectic is untenable with regard to racial slavery. As he notes in a remarkable footnote that rips the master-slave dialectic asunder, "I hope I have shown that here the master differs basically from the master described by Hegel. For Hegel there is reciprocity; here the master laughs at the consciousness of the slave. What he wants from the slave is not recognition but work."[30]

But what does the slave want? Here I would argue that Fanon is ambiguous and that he gets the historical record of slave revolts in the Caribbean wrong due to his narrow focus on French-speaking islands, which excludes Haiti. Fanon is very specific in addressing French abolitionism. He is not referring to abolitionism in general when he notes, "the black man contented himself with thanking the white man, and the most forceful proof of the fact is the impressive number of statues erected all over France and the colonies to show the white France stroking the kinky hair of this nice Negro whose chains had just been broken."[31] Fanon has French abolitionism in mind when he says, "The White man, in the capacity of master, said to the Negro, 'From now on you are free.'"[32] He continues, "But the Negro knows nothing of the cost of freedom for he has not fought for it. From time to time he has fought for liberty and justice, but these were always white liberty and white justice."[33] For Fanon the slave desires "to be like the master. . . . in Hegel the slave turns away from the master and turns toward the object. Here the slave turns towards the master and abandons the object."[34] This is a strange reading of slave emancipation by Fanon. He is very accurate to point to French and, I would argue, British and American abolitionism as very much about white liberty and white justice. But this was not the only strain of abolitionism. There was a black abolitionism that carried within itself a logic of liberation as the ground of freedom. The most important expression of this current of abolitionism occurred in the dual Haitian Revolution.[35] Any examination of this revolution illustrates that Fanon is accurate about the master's only wishing work from the slave but that Fanon is wrong about what the slave wants. I would argue that the slave turns away from the object of work but does not turn toward the master. Instead the slave turns to a series of practices of freedom.[36] For the slave, the nature of slave labor that uses both the slave and labor as chattel means that one effective practice of freedom is the negation of plantation labor. Thus the slave in the Atlantic world neither functions, as Alexandre Kojeve says, as a part of the master's "existential impasse,"[37] nor does the slave want to be like the master. The slave primarily turns his face away from work toward the master in order to remove the master as the source of domination. The slave does this to break the bondage of enslavement and to find a new freedom.

In a path-breaking study of the slave dimension of the Haitian revolution, Carolyn Fick tells us about an observation by a French colonial official who was perturbed at the actions of ex-slaves. She writes that the official became preoccupied and noticed that the ex-slaves were, in his words, "unambitious and uncompetitive, the black values his liberty only to the extent that it affords him the possibility of living according to his own philosophy."[38] The question before us, one that we have yet to fully grapple with, is, what was this philosophy of freedom? In my view, this is the question that is posed when we not only decenter Western thought but also change our gaze. But let us return to *Black Skin, White Masks*.

We are now in a position to pursue further Fanon's reading of Hegel's master-slave dialectic as buttressed by historical events: The master wants the slave to work and desires recognition only to the extent that it will make the slave work. The slave wants freedom and faces the master to destroy the system of slavery. This is a new dialectic, neither one of recognition nor one of unequal encounter, but one in which new forms of freedom are being imagined, plotted, and enacted wherever possible.

What does this have to do with critical thought? Everything. I would argue that this new dialectic can best be seen in the dual Haitian Revolution and the ways in which practices of freedom played themselves out during the process of that revolution.[39] I want therefore to suggest that in the end one vital resource for us in the development of critical thought is the character of the slave's freedom, which emerged in distinct opposition to the liberties of those who ruled the Atlantic world in the eighteenth century. Space does not allow a full elaboration of this point, but one of the issues raised in the dual Haitian Revolution was the relationship of wage labor to freedom.[40] This was part of the ex-slave's own philosophy. The ex-slave's reluctance in becoming a wage laborer means that long before Marx discerned that wage labor was really "wage slavery," the Haitian ex-slave recognized this. Thus issues of freedom arising from the perspective of the ex-slave should not be separated into distinct spheres; they are closely tied into a knot about how to live. The ex-slaves may not have found the answer to this question, but it is the posing that we are concerned with.

I am not arguing here that slave freedom is in any way a model of freedom for our present moment. I also eschew thinking in models because I think it is a dangerous exercise, reducing the complexities of human action to narrow slots. What I am suggesting is that the practices of slave freedom pose the following questions for us today:

- What is the relationship between freedom and labor or work?
- What is the relationship between equality and freedom? Are these irrevocably separate ends?
- How do human societies construct ways of life in which human domination does not factor?

A reader may say that some of these questions have already been posed in various ways and in different traditions. And my response would be yes. But the dual Haitian Revolution posed all three simultaneously. So while other revolutions of the period marked partial ruptures, the dual Haitian Revolution exploded into new terrain. Such ruptures, though robust, also tend to be fragile, and we often lose sight of the questions posed by the practices of those who wish to turn liberation into freedom. Fanon recognizes this.

In the conclusion to *Black Skin, White Masks*, Fanon invokes Marx by paying attention to the character of a social revolution. Marx made the point that the "social revolution . . . cannot draw its poetry from the past but only from the future, thereby creating a situation where content exceeds its expression."[41] This is the central idea upon which Fanon builds the concluding chapter of *Black Skin, White Masks*. Without making any explicit reference to Aimé

Césaire's classic poem *Notebook of a Return to My Native Land* and its assumptions about the burden of history, Fanon critiques Césaire's understanding of the function of history in the colonial context as a nightmare in which the colonized encounters a past haunted by deep pain. Césaire's poem rejects this pain and constructs in its place a desire that embraces history, but not the history manufactured by the colonial power. He writes in *Notebook*:

> Eia for those who have never invented anything
> For those who have never explored anything
> For those who have never subdued anything.[42]

However, for Fanon the nightmare of colonial history was a burden that trapped the struggle for freedom. As he forcefully proclaims, "Like it or not, the past cannot in no way guide me in the present moment."[43] Of course Fanon is writing polemically here because he has in mind a certain view of history that in his view seeks to represent Africa in terms that mask particular African historical realities. However, there is no doubt that Fanon is ambiguous about history, about its function and relationship to acts of emancipation, so that oftentimes he gestures and calls upon us to move beyond the historical. And here I both disagree and agree. If Fanon means that the past is superseded and dead, then I disagree. If he means that the past must not be a burden but a release, then I am in agreement. History in the present is not about burden or mourning; it is about accounting for the population of the dead. But this dead population is not dead, because their actions leave traces that work to configure the world. In this sense our present historical actions are dialogues between the living and the dead. This is why the questions of history are always about the present. To engage in this dialogue we remember wounds, but more importantly, we hear the cries produced by wounds. Those cries affirm a different kind of freedom; they point us to a different song of the future upon which we can draw. But we draw from these future songs with a sense of history. Of course this is not a "monumentalistic conception of the past," but rather a critical history, what I have called elsewhere a "dread history."[44] Fanon recognizes this because he writes, just before he concludes the final chapter of *Black Skin, White Masks*:

> The self takes its place by opposing itself; Yes and No. I said in my introduction that man is a yes, I will never stop reiterating that. *Yes* to life. *Yes* to Love. *Yes* to generosity. But man is also a *no*. *No* to the scorn of man. *No* to the degradation of man. *No* to the exploitation of man. *No* to the butchery of what is most human in man: freedom.[45]

Fanon's affirmations are key to my arguments here because he uses them to establish a possible trajectory for critical thought and praxis. So in the last four pages of his text, he returns to history and writes, "I am not a prisoner of history. I should not seek there the meaning of my destiny. I should constantly remind myself that the real *leap* consists in introducing invention into existence. In the world through which I travel, I am endlessly creating myself."[46] These are remarkable sentences. What do they mean, and how can we think with them?

First there is the drama of life itself: it is about endlessly creating oneself. This drama suggests that one element of freedom might include establishing the conditions under which creation is possible. So if freedom is about creation (not self-realization), Fanon does not separate the *conditions for* and the *exercise of* freedom. Second, although ambiguous about history, Fanon wants us to consider that living is not simply about existence. For Fanon it is not enough to say that existence is ontologically prior to essence because of the facticity of being in the world. *To be is to live and to live is to invent, to create with others.* So the capacity to create is *the* active part of being. The conditions for this creativity simultaneously construct grounds for the leap of invention and create the grounds of and for the practice of freedom itself. These practices allow us to go beyond being. Fanon writes, "I am a part of Being to the degree that

I go beyond it."[47] In going beyond being, Fanon states that we negate the hierarchies human societies have constructed and instead make attempts "to touch each other, to feel each other, to explain the other to myself."[48] In Fanon's call all hierarchies are flattened, the other is no longer an Other, and a common ground of being human is established by which we may live together and construct humane ways of life. Fanon then ends with a sentence that with one stroke reworks liberal theory. With a force rarely seen in political literature, he asks, "Was my freedom not given to me then in order to build the world of the *You*?"[49] There is no more Other or I, as a common humanity in all its pluralism and difference becomes the foundation for critical thought and radical political praxis.

Fanon then outlines a perspective that we in our old penchant for labels would call "radical humanism."[50] So for the sake of this lecture let us call it that. This is a humanism in which the critical element of being human is the degree to which one is part of being and yet is able to go beyond it to build the world of the You. This is not a humanism in which the human, though central, is conceived of as a "whole series of subjected sovereignties [and] a theory of the subject," as Michel Foucault tells us.[51] In Western thought humanism is very much a discourse about the human and the possibilities of mastery of self. In Marxist theory, humanism is about ending estranged labor that alienates the worker from the human self.[52] Fanon and other radical anticolonial thinkers do not present either of these conceptions of humanism. Rather, their affirmation of the human rejects conventional humanist discourse to develop a radical politics of the human in which human beings are neither ends nor means. To be human is to live, to engage in a set of practices of inventions that creates freedom. In such a form of life, reason is also deeply connected to the body as the force that enacts these practices and is their embodiment. No wonder Fanon ends the chapter and the book with the cry: "My final prayer: O my body, make of me always a man who questions."[53]

In Fanon's thought Europe's colonial project disqualifies it from leading a new radical enterprise. Thus he issues his call in the final sentences of *The Wretched of the Earth* in which he proclaims, "For Europe, for ourselves, and for humanity, comrades, we must turn over a new leaf, we must work out new concepts, and try and set afoot a new man."[54] The issues now emerge: Where are these concepts to come from? How may we think about them and their relationship to critical thought and critical theory?

In general, critical theory can loosely be described as "a whole range of theories which take a critical view of society and the human sciences or which seek to explain the emergence of their objects of knowledge."[55] Of course the work of the Frankfurt School has been central to this tradition.[56] I want to argue that an overarching purpose of both critical thought and critical theory has been to critique the workings of power, to mark the shifts of power and its new configurations, and to make clear its dominant apparatuses and capacities. This intellectual labor continues to be a necessary feature of critical thought, and to some degree these lectures have operated in this tradition. However, if we think about other possible meanings of Walter Benjamin's phrase "the traditions of the oppressed," we notice another productive element to critical thought that is often not paid attention to: the opening up of another archive in which power is contested. This is not about writing a new history of resistance, or even of revolution, but about developing a capacity to gaze on practices through which we may grasp how different acts of humanization occur.

I hope that by now you are beginning to see the outline of what I am working through. I am traversing a different terrain, not one that gets caught up with forms of democracy or theories of social change (important as these are), but rather a terrain that asks us to think about *what we are, what we have become, and how we might rupture the frames of our present selves.* How do we create a rupture in which the profound questions opened up by colonial and racial power are both posed and, if possible, answered? How do we live together in difference? How do we construct ways of life that create a human world of a *You*, not of an *other*?

These questions appear before us in sharp focus because the empire of liberty seeks an end of history in which different possibilities of the human are closed off. The issues I have raised open a critical intellectual space both to imagine new possibilities and to gain a historical sense of various forms of life. In other words, I suggest that critical thought can become productive by focusing not just on power but on *ways and forms of life*. By this I mean practices in which thinking is both thought and doing. This is a form of activity that may move us beyond a consideration of being as only ontology and into a space where existence is about ways of life. I submit that power today understands this. In Arendt's words, power understands that politics is not only about the "co-existence and association of different men," but is about the ways of life constructed in this association. Politics is about ways of life constituting life forms, what the Jamaican Rastafari calls *livity*.

The current objective of power is to construct a "politics of being," to preserve life as it is, to stop action and foreclose possibility, since the human world is our own artifice. To reinvent action requires us to move beyond this "politics of being" to *a politics of the radical imagination.* Such a politics functions in two ways. First, it deciphers the codes of power, and second, it allows us to think outside the death-drive of power. It allows us to construct freedom not as an absolute but as an ever-changing contingency of our fragile imperfectibility. I wish to end this lecture with a series of statements:

- We live today at a peculiar moment in human history in which *free-dom* has become the sign of human domination.
- We live today at a moment when violence and torture are performed in various places with a kind of banality, while the dialogue we engage in concerns degrees of pain and what constitutes punishment and torture.

- We live in a world in which the traces of the colonial modern are not just haunting shadows but are part of the everyday technologies of rule that are deployed.
- We live in a world in which the traces of racial domination continue to shape our human world.
- We live in a world in which we have yet to face the most complex questions posed by the event of the colonial encounter: How shall we live together in difference? What does freedom look like when we bring "invention into existence"?

I offer no immediate answers to these questions, not because there are none, but because answers for life and living can only be found in the practices of life itself and in our theorization of those practices. I hope that in this lecture series I have been able to open a conversation, to pose a few questions, and in the end to ask all of us to heed the cries of wounds that have emerged from various historical events, so that perhaps in our fragile lives we may construct freedom. A freedom in which we constitute our humanness.

NOTES

Introduction

1. Stuart Hall, "The Toad in the Garden: Thatcherism among the Theorists," in *Marxism and the Interpretation of Culture*, ed. Cary Nelson and Lawrence Grossberg (Urbana: University of Illinois Press, 1988), p. 49.

2. C. L. R. James, *The Future in the Present* (London: Allison and Busby, 1977), pp. 202–3.

3. These essays have been published in Anthony Bogues, *Black Heretics, Black Prophets: Radical Political Intellectuals* (New York: Routledge, 2003).

4. E-mail exchange with Ronald Judy, August 2009.

5. Of course I here refer to the way in which Michel Foucault uses the term to describe the emergence of a new form of power which seeks to capture "man-as-species." Later on I will expand this conception and argue that the current drive of power is about capturing human desires and imagination. For Foucault's discussion of the bio-political, see Michel Foucault, *"Society Must Be Defended": Lectures at the Collège de France, 1975–1976*, ed. Mauro Bertani and Alessandro Fontana, trans. David Macey (New York: Picador, 2003), chapter 11.

6. Cited in Robert W. Tucker and David Hendrickson, *Empire of Liberty: The Statecraft of Thomas Jefferson* (Oxford: Oxford University Press, 1990), p. 159.

7. W. E. B. DuBois, *Black Reconstruction in America: An Essay Toward a History of the Part Which Black Folk Played in the Attempt to Reconstruct Democracy in America, 1860–1880* (New York: Atheneum, 1962), p. 3.

8. Jacques Rancière, *Hatred of Democracy* (London: Verso, 2006), p. 3.

Chapter 1: Empire of Liberty

1. Selected examples of this debate appear in the following: Niall Ferguson, *Colossus: The Price of America's Empire* (New York: Penguin Press, 2004);

Joseph Nye, Jr., *The Paradox of American Power* (Oxford: Oxford University Press, 2002); Andrew J. Bacevich, ed., *The Imperial Tense: Prospects and Problems of American Empire* (Chicago: Ivan R. Dee, 2003); Amy Kaplan, *The Anarchy of Empire in the Making of U.S. Culture* (Cambridge, MA: Harvard University Press, 2002); Andrew J. Bacevich, *American Empire: The Realities and Consequences of U.S. Diplomacy* (Cambridge, MA: Harvard University Press, 2002). We also need to be reminded that there has always been an anti-imperialist tradition in American life. For books and discussions about some elements of this tradition, see the Web site: www.americanempireproject .com.

2. For a sense of the issues involved in this side of the debate, see the essays in *Daedalus*, Spring 2005.

3. The most important argument along these lines is Michael Ignatieff, "The American Empire: The Burden," *New York Times*, May 5, 2003.

4. Michael Hardt and Antonio Negri, *Empire* (Cambridge, MA: Harvard University Press, 2000), p. 9.

5. Ibid.

6. Dominic Lieven, *Empire: The Russian Empire and Its Rivals* (London: John Murray, 2000), p. 14.

7. Pierre Manent, *An Intellectual History of Liberalism*, trans. Rebecca Balinski (Princeton, NJ: Princeton University Press, 1995), p. 3.

8. Ibid.

9. Of course there are the additional questions of the conceptual basis of a universal human nature and of what constitutes imperial legitimacy. To put the matter bluntly, on what basis and under what assumptions is the good in the political realm conceptualized?

10. Cited in Anthony Pagden, *Peoples and Empires* (New York: Modern Library, 2001), p. 26.

11. Ibid., p. 29.

12. Thus many supporters of American empire have pointed out America's reluctance to engage in what is called nation building. For a discussion of this, see Ferguson, *Colossus*.

13. Cited in Robert Aldrich, *The Age of Empires* (London, Thames and Hudson, 2002), 302.

14. Cited in Eric Foner, *The Story of American Freedom* (New York: Norton, 1998), p. 9.

15. Cited in Tucker and Hendrickson, *Empire of Liberty*, p. 19.

16. Julian Boyd, "Thomas Jefferson's 'Empire of Liberty'" *Virginia Quarterly Review*, no. 24 (1948): p. 548.

17. Tucker and Hendrickson, *Empire of Liberty*, p. 7.

18. Cited in Amy Kaplan, "Violent Belonging and the Question of Empire Today" (Presidential Address to the American Studies Association) *American Quarterly* 56, no. 1 (March 2004): p. 5.

19. Cited in Aldrich, *Age of Empires*, p. 280.

20. Cited in Aldrich, *Age of Empires*, p. 280.

21. For a discussion of these interventions, see Jenny Pearce, *Under the Eagle: U.S. Intervention in Latin America and the Caribbean* (Boston: South End Press, 1982).

22. William Appleman Williams, *Empire as a Way of Life* (Oxford: Oxford University Press, 1980).

23. Hannah Arendt, *The Human Condition* (Chicago: University of Chicago Press, 1998), p. 7.

24. Foucault, *"Society Must Be Defended,"* p. 242.

25. Ibid., p. 245.

26. Michel Foucault, "The Subject and Power," in *Power* (New York: New Press, 2000), p. 332.

27. Ibid., p. 333.

28. Ibid.

29. William Leach, *Land of Desire: Merchants, Power, and the Rise of a New American Culture* (New York: Vintage, 1994), p. 6.

30. Ibid., p. 8.

31. Cited in Leach, *Land of Desire*, p. 37.

32. Ibid.

33. Achille Mbembe, *On Private Indirect Government* (Dakar: CODESRIA, 2000), p. 7.

34. Raymond Williams, *Keywords: A Vocabulary of Culture and Society* (Oxford: Oxford University Press, 1983), p. 57.

35. Alice Conklin, *A Mission to Civilize: The Republican Idea of Empire in France and West Africa, 1895–1930* (Stanford, CA: Stanford University Press, 1997), p. 1.

36. Ibid., p. 13.

37. It is interesting to read many of the debates over the implementation of French colonial power, particularly over the project of colonization in Algeria. See the 1841 essay in Jennifer Pitts, ed. and trans., *Alexis de Tocqueville: Writings on Empire and Slavery* (Baltimore: Johns Hopkins University Press, 2001), pp. 59–116. Tocqueville argued about the relationship of domination to colonization and in his 1841 essay on Algeria made the point that "domination . . . is the only means to achieve colonization" (p. 64). For Tocqueville, domination was about war, but colonialism was in part about a civilizing mission.

38. Frantz Fanon, *Black Skin, White Masks* (New York: Grove Press, 1967), pp. 17–18.

39. For a discussion of this process and the ways in which British colonial policy executed its civilizing mission in a post-slavery context, see Thomas Holt, *The Problem of Freedom* (Kingston, Jamaica: Ian Randle Press, 1992). See also Catherine Hall, *Civilizing Subjects* (Chicago: University of Chicago Press, 2002).

40. For a discussion of Mill's ideas on race and colonialism, see Anthony Bogues, "John Stuart Mill and 'The Negro Question': Race, Colonialism, and the Ladder of Civilization," in Andrew Valls, ed., *Race and Racism in Modern Philosophy* (Ithaca, NY: Cornell University Press, 2005), pp. 217–34.

41. Cited in Niall Ferguson, "The unconscious colossus: limits of (& alternatives to) American empire" *Daedalus* 134, no. 2 (Spring 2005): p. 22.

42. Sacvan Bercovitch, *The American Jeremiad* (Madison: University of Wisconsin Press, 1978), pp. 93–94.

43. John Gray, *Two Faces of Liberalism* (New York: New Press, 2000), p. 2.

44. Robert Cooper, "Imperial Liberalism," *The National Interest*, no. 79 (Spring 2005): p. 34.

45. Louis Althusser, "Ideology and the Ideological State Apparatuses," in *Lenin and Philosophy and Other Essays* (New York: Monthly Review Press, 2001), p. 116.

46. Ibid.

47. Raymond Williams, *The Long Revolution* (Peterborough, Ontario: Broadview Press, 2001), p. 64.

48. George Bush, "America's Responsibility, America's Mission," in *Imperial Tense* (see note 8), p. 5.

49. Jacques Lacan, *Ecrits: A Selection* (New York: Norton, 2004), p. 330.

50. For a discussion of this idea, see Sylvia Wynter, "On How We Mistook the Map for the Territory, and Re-Imprisoned Ourselves in Our Unbearable Wrongness of Being, of *Désêtre*: Black Studies Toward the Human Project," in *Not Only the Master's Tools: African-American Studies in Theory and Practice*, ed. Lewis R. Gordon and Jane Anna Gordon (Boulder, CO: Paradigm Press, 2006), pp. 107–69.

51. For a discussion of this, see Zygmunt Bauman, *Consuming Life* (Cambridge: Polity Press, 2007).

52. J. A. Hobson, *Imperialism* (New York: Gordon Press, 1975), p. 23.

53. See in particular Harry Magdoff, *Imperialism without Colonies* (New York: Monthly Review Press, 2003).

54. Of course there are American colonies, and the history of American intervention in Latin America is one in which military and authoritarian dictatorships were openly helped and supported.

55. Rogers Smith, *Civic Ideals* (New Haven, CT: Yale University Press, 1997), p. 6.

56. Judith Shklar, "Positive Liberty, Negative Liberty in the United States," in *Redeeming American Political Thought* (Chicago: University of Chicago Press, 1998), p. 111.

57. Cited in J. H. Elliott, *Empires of the Atlantic World: Britain and Spain in America, 1492–1830* (New Haven, CT: Yale University Press, 2006), pp. 9–10.

58. Ibid., p. 12.

59. See in particular Donald Pease, "9/11: When Was 'American Studies After the New Americanists'?" *boundary* 2 33, no. 3 (Fall 2006): pp. 73–101.

60. Sheldon Wolin, *Politics and Vision* (Princeton, NJ: Princeton University Press, 2004), p. 590.

61. See Giorgio Agamben, *State of Exception* (Chicago: University of Chicago Press, 2005).

62. One intellectual current that I do not deal with in this lecture is that of American exceptionalism. There are many texts on this subject. I recommend two: William Spanos, *American Exceptionalism in the Age of Globalization* (Albany: State University of New York Press, 2008), and, more recently, Donald Pease, *New American Exceptionalism* (Minneapolis: University of Minnesota Press, 2009).

63. Elsa Goveia, *The West Indian Slave Laws of the 18th Century* (Bridgetown, Barbados: Caribbean Universities Press, 1970), p. 21.

64. Joan Dayan, "Legal Slaves and Civil Bodies," in *Materializing Democracy: Toward a Revitalized Cultural Politics*, ed. Russ Castronovo and Dana Nelson (Durham, NC: Duke University Press, 2002), p. 55.

65. Cited in A. Leon Higginbotham, Jr., *In the Matter of Color: Race and the American Legal Process* (Oxford: Oxford University Press, 1978), p. 163.

66. Ibid., p. 39.

67. Nicolás Guillén, *Man-Making Words: Selected Poems of Nicolás Guillén*, trans. Roberto Márquez and David McMurray (Amherst: University of Massachusetts Press, 1972), p. 187.

68. For an initial discussion of this subject, see Anthony Bogues, *Singing Songs of Freedom* (forthcoming).

69. Foucault, *"Society Must Be Defended,"* p. 240.

70. Giorgio Agamben, *Homo Sacer: Sovereign Power and Bare Life* (Stanford, CA: Stanford University Press, 1998).

71. Perhaps one way to think of this is to complicate our understanding of modernity by thinking about it as colonial modernity. In other words, we ought to grapple with the fact that we cannot think historically about so-called modernity itself without locating it alongside colonial rule and therefore coloniality.

72. Colin Dayan, "Legal Terrors" *Representations*, no. 92 (Fall 2005): p. 49.

73. Colin Dayan, "Cruel and Unusual: The End of the Eighth Amendment" *Boston Review*, November 2004, http://www.bostonreview.net/BR 29.5/dayan .php. My initial argument uses a great deal from Colin Dayan's current work on this subject.

74. Karen J. Greenberg and Joshua L. Dratel, eds., *The Torture Papers: The Road to Abu Ghraib* (New York: Cambridge University Press, 2005), p. 53.

75. This is simply untrue. I have profound disagreements with the rubric of "failed state," but any cursory glance at the states labeled in this way demonstrates that many of them have seats in the UN, a sure marker of international recognition.

76. I have summarized the conditions for a failed state as outlined by the document. For a full description, see Karen J. Greenberg and Joshua Dratel, *The Torture Papers: The Road to Abu Ghraib* (Cambridge: Cambridge University Press, 2005), pp. 38–125.

77. Cited in Christina Burnett and Burke Marshall, eds., *Foreign in a Domestic Sense* (Durham, NC: Duke University Press, 2001), p. 13.

78. Cited in Kaplan, *Anarchy of Empire*, p. 10.

79. See Charles Mills, *The Racial Contract* (Ithaca, NY: Cornell University Press, 1997).

80. Cited in David Hackett Fischer, *Liberty and Freedom: A Visual History of America's Founding Ideas* (Oxford: Oxford University Press, 2005), p. 715.

81. Pierre Bourdieu, *Language and Symbolic Power* (Cambridge, MA: Harvard University Press, 1995), p. 23.

82. Ibid.

83. Foucault, *"Society Must Be Defended,"* p. 246.

84. Graham Burchell, "Peculiar Interests: Civil Society and Governing 'The System of Natural Liberty,'" in *The Foucault Effect: Studies in Governmentality*, ed. Graham Burchell, Colin Gordon, and Peter Miller (Chicago: University of Chicago Press, 1999), p. 139.

85. Langston Hughes, "Words Like Freedom," in *The Collected Poems of Langston Hughes*, ed. Arnold Rampersad and David Roessel (New York: Vintage, 1995), p. 269.

Chapter 2: Race, Historical Trauma, and Democracy

1. Saidiya Hartman, *Scenes of Subjection* (New York: Oxford University Press, 1997), p. 3.

2. Ibid.

3. Frantz Fanon, *Black Skin, White Masks* (New York: Grove Press, 1967), p. 8.

4. Dominick LaCapra, *Writing History, Writing Trauma* (Baltimore: Johns Hopkins University Press, 2001), p. 81.

5. When I use the word *wrong* here, I mean it in some of the senses in which Jacques Rancière deploys it. See Jacques Rancière, *Disagreement: Politics and Philosophy* (Minneapolis: University of Minnesota Press, 1999), especially chapter 2. For Rancière, "the wrong is simply the mode of subjectification in which the assertion of equality takes its political shape." p. 39. However, I also wish to use the word in the sense that a wrong runs counter to justice. A historical wrong therefore is one in which issues of justice are erased from the enacted event. This means that there is no shadow of justice that haunts the event, because those wronged are said to have no claims on justice.

6. Cathy Caruth, *Unclaimed Experience: Trauma, Narrative, and History* (Baltimore: Johns Hopkins University Press, 1996), pp. 3–4.

7. Ruth Leys, *Trauma: A Genealogy* (Chicago: University of Chicago Press, 2000), p. 2.

8. Ibid.

9. See Ron Eyerman, *Cultural Trauma: Slavery and the Formation of African American Identity* (Cambridge: Cambridge University Press, 2001), pp. 2–4.

10. Toni Morrison, "The Site of Memory," in *Inventing the Truth: The Art and Craft of Memoir*, ed. William Zinsser (Boston: Mariner Books, 1998), pp. 190–91.

11. Sigmund Freud, *Beyond the Pleasure Principle* (New York: Norton, 1989), p. 11.

12. For a discussion of this, see Stephanie Smallwood, *Saltwater Slavery: A Middle Passage from Africa to American Diaspora* (Cambridge, MA: Harvard University Press, 2007), pp. 1–8.

13. Ibid., p. 152.

14. For a discussion of this tradition and its radical expressions, see Cedric Robinson, *Black Marxism: The Making of the Black Radical Tradition* (London: Zed Press, 1983).

15. LaCapra, *Writing History, Writing Trauma*, p. 77.

16. Ibid., p. 78.

17. Smallwood, *Saltwater Slavery*, p. 60.

18. Robert Gooding-Williams, *Look, A Negro: Philosophical Essays on Race, Culture and Politics* (New York: Routledge, 2006), p. 1.

19. Fanon, *Black Skin, White Masks*.

20. Glenn Loury, "Ghettoes, Prisons and Racial Stigma" (The Tanner Lectures, April 4, 2007), copy provided by author.

21. Howard Winant, *The New Politics of Race* (Minneapolis: University of Minnesota Press, 2004), p. 11.

22. *How Race Is Lived in America* (New York: Times Books, 2001), p. 26.

23. Fanon, *Black Skin, White Masks*, p. 112.

24. W. E. B. DuBois, *The Souls of Black Folk* (New York: Dodd, Mead and Company, 1961), p. 1.

25. Donald Pease, "Tocqueville's Democratic Thing; or, Aristocracy in America," in *Materializing Democracy: Toward a Revitalized Cultural Politics*, ed. Russ Castronovo and Dana Nelson (Durham, NC: Duke University Press, 2002), p. 23.

26. Ibid.

27. Alexis de Tocqueville, *Democracy in America*, vol. 1 (New York: Vintage, 1990), p. 19.

28. Ibid., p. 3.

29. Alexis de Tocqueville, *Democracy in America*, ed. J. P. Mayer, trans. George Lawrence, 2 vols. (New York: Perennial, 2000), p. 504.

30. Sheldon Wolin, *Tocqueville between Two Worlds: The Making of a Political and Theoretical Life* (Princeton, NJ: Princeton University Press, 2001), p. 241.

31. Cited in Wolin, *Tocqueville between Two Worlds*, p. 251.

32. Tocqueville, *Democracy in America*, vol. 1 (New York: Vintage, 1990), p. 9.

33. For a selection of Tocqueville's writings on colonial empire, see Pitts, *Alexis de Tocqueville: Writings on Empire and Slavery*.

34. Ibid., p. 200.

35. Ibid., p. 203.

36. Ibid., pp. 207–8.

37. See Gustave de Beaumont, *Marie or, Slavery in the United States*, trans. Barbara Chapman, with a new introduction by Gerard Fergerson (Baltimore: Johns Hopkins University Press, 1999). In the introduction to *Democracy in America*, Tocqueville makes reference to the work of his companion during his visit to America, Gustave de Beaumont. While Beaumont's novel and its sociological appendixes explicitly argue that slavery was a negation of equality and democracy in the U.S. and was therefore not an incidental issue, Tocqueville was not influenced by this position. It confirms that he was committed to ideas from philosophical anthropology about the human race that were constructed upon a hierarchy of white superiority. In his text, Beaumont provides a brief discussion of American women, as well as a short essay on social and political equality in the U.S. and the role of white skin as a marker of privilege.

38. Tocqueville, *Democracy in America*, vol. 1 (New York: Vintage, 1990), p. 331.

39. Ibid.

40. Ibid., p. 332.

41. Ibid.

42. Ibid., p. 333.

43. Ibid., p. 358.

44. Ibid., p. 373.

45. The ACS was formed with the explicit purpose of raising funds and formulating a plan to return free blacks to Africa. The driving idea behind the plan was a growing fear of free blacks. Although some members of the organization opposed slavery, race was the primary motive. Henry Clay noted that because of the unconquerable prejudice resulting from their color, blacks never could amalgamate with the free whites of this country. Some white abolitionists agreed, and some blacks also agreed. However, most organizations of free blacks opposed the plan, and Frederick Douglass was in fierce opposition to it.

46. Nikhil Pal Singh, *Black Is a Country* (Cambridge, MA: Harvard University Press, 2004), p. 92. It should be noted here that, while some historians have attempted to build upon the work of DuBois in *Black Reconstruction*, the text is still little studied. Besides Singh, see Cedric Robinson's *Black Marxism* (London: Zed Press, 1987), in particular chapter 9.

47. Cited in Singh, *Black Is a Country*, p. 95.

48. W. E. B. DuBois, *Black Reconstruction*, p. 727.

49. Ibid., p. 3.

50. Ibid., p. 5.

51. Ibid., pp. 9–10.

52. C. L. R. James, *The Black Jacobins* (New York: Vintage, 1989), pp. 85–86.

53. Rancière, *Disagreement*, p. 11.

54. Dubois, *Black Reconstruction*, p. 67.

55. Ibid., pp. 122–23.

56. Hannah Arendt, *On Revolution* (London: Penguin, 1965), p. 21.

57. Ibid.

58. Ibid., p. 68.

59. Ibid., p. 71.

60. Dubois, *Black Reconstruction*, p. 124.

61. Ibid., p. 13.

62. Ibid., p. 182.

63. Ibid.

64. Ibid., p. 185.

65. W. E. B. DuBois, "Marxism and the Negro Problem," in *W. E. B. Du Bois: A Reader*, ed. David Levering Lewis (New York: Henry Holt and Company, 1995), p. 543.

66. John Dunn, "Conclusion," in *Democracy: The Unfinished Journey, 508 BC to AD 1993*, ed. John Dunn (Oxford: Oxford University Press, 1993), pp. 240–41.

67. We of course need to acknowledge that this citizen self-rule was itself limited to men and that Athens was a slave society. For a discussion of this fact and the conceptions of slavery in both Athens and Rome, see Moses Finley, *Ancient Slavery and Modern Ideology* (Princeton, NJ: Markus Wiener Publishers, 1998).

68. Ernesto Laclau, *Emancipation(s)* (London: Verso, 1996), p. 102.

69. The Levellers, *The Putney Debates*, with an introduction by Geoffrey Robertson (London: Verso, 2007), p. 52.

70. Ibid., p. 53.

71. Stuart Hall, ed., *Representation: Cultural Representations and Signifying Practices* (London: Sage Publications, 2003), p. 19.

72. Ella Baker, "Bigger than a Hamburger," *The Southern Patriot*, May 1960.

73. Jacques Rancière, *On the Shores of Politics* (London: Verso, 1995), p. 103.

Chapter 3: Death, Power, Violence, and New Sovereignties

1. Jean Hatzfeld, *Machete Season: The Killers in Rwanda Speak* (New York: Picador, 2003), p. 10.

2. For example, see his recently published notes on Tasmania taken from his proposed unwritten book on the history of genocide. The section on Tasmania is published as Raphael Lemkin, "Tasmania," in *Colonialism and Genocide*, ed. A. Dirk Moses and Dan Stone (London: Routledge, 2007), pp. 74–100.

3. Hannah Arendt, *The Origins of Totalitarianism* (New York: Harvest/HBJ Books, 1973), p. 461.

4. One of the most important texts to discuss this point is Mahmood Mamdani, *When Victims Become Killers: Colonialism, Nativism, and the Genocide in Rwanda* (Princeton, NJ: Princeton University Press, 2001).

5. Hatzfeld, *Machete Season*, p. 7.

6. See Jürgen Zimmerer, "The birth of the *Ostland* out of the spirit of colonialism: a postcolonial perspective on the Nazi policy of conquest and extermination," in Moses and Stone, *Colonialism and Genocide* (see note 2 above), pp. 101–23, for a discussion of this German general and how the military tactics in his genocidal campaign against the Herero were repeated by the Nazis.

7. Hatzfeld, *Machete Season*, p. 13.

8. Hannah Arendt, *Eichmann in Jerusalem*, in Peter Baehr, ed., *The Portable Hannah Arendt* (New York: Penguin, 2000), p. 328.

9. Hatzfeld, *Machete Season*, p. 15.

10. Hannah Arendt, "The Image of Hell," in *Essays in Understanding*, ed. Jerome Kohn (New York: Schocken Books, 1994), p. 198.

11. Primo Levi, *The Voice of Memory: Interviews, 1961–1987*, ed. Marco Belpoliti and Robert Gordon (New York: New Press, 2001), p. 195.

12. Ibid., p. 202.

13. Hannah Arendt, *On Violence* (New York: Harcourt, Brace, and Company, 1969), p. 56.

14. Ibid., p. 65. I would suggest that a close reading of Arendt's criticism of Fanon illustrates that she is really reading the text through Sartre's introduction to the text.

15. Mary Douglas, "The Two Bodies," in *The Body: A Reader*, ed. Mariam Fraser and Monica Greco (New York: Routledge, 2005), p. 79.

16. Elaine Scarry, *The Body in Pain* (Oxford: Oxford University Press, 1985), p. 34.

17. Ibid.

18. Cited in Steven Lukes, ed., *Power* (New York: New York University Press, 1986), p. 4.

19. Michel Foucault, "The Subject and Power," in *Power*, ed. James Faubion (New York: New Press, 2000), p. 337.

20. Ibid., p. 340.

21. Judith Shklar, "Putting Cruelty First" *Daedalus* 111, no. 3 (Summer 1982): pp. 17–28.

22. Ibid.

23. See in particular the debate between Jean Bethke Elshtain and Michael Walzer in Sanford Levinson, ed., *Torture: A Collection* (Oxford: Oxford University Press, 2004), pp. 61–92.

24. David Luban, "Liberalism, Torture, and the Ticking Bomb," in *The Torture Debate in America*, ed. Karen J. Greenberg (Cambridge: Cambridge University Press, 2006), p. 36.

25. Ibid., p. 38.

26. Cited in Luban, "Liberalism, Torture, and the Ticking Bomb," p. 75.

27. See the document in Karen Greenberg and Joshua Dratel, *The Torture Papers: The Road to Abu Ghraib* (Cambridge: Cambridge University Press, 2005), p. 237.

28. Michel Foucault, *Discipline and Punish: The Birth of the Prison* (New York: Vintage, 1995), p. 9.

29. Ibid., p. 11.

30. I would also argue that, because this is so, when placed in pain these excluded bodies can be made a spectacle of. In the twenty-first century, although there is no public spectacle of punishment in liberal societies, the visual recording of torture substitutes for this spectacle because pictures can be shown widely. The use of photography in public spectacles of torture and death has a long history in the United States, including the numerous pictures of lynched

slaves and ex-slaves taken and sent to friends and family by those who witnessed the enactment of lynching. The pictures of Abu Ghraib followed this established practice.

31. Greenberg and Dratel, *Torture Papers*, p. 55.

32. Colin Dayan, *The Story of Cruel and Unusual* (Cambridge, MA: MIT Press, 2007), p. xv.

33. Ibid., p. 16.

34. The debates also ignore another ghost, the historical involvement of the U.S. government in practices of torture in Latin America. For a discussion of these extensive practices, see Jennifer Harbury, *Truth, Torture and the American Way* (Boston: Beacon Press, 2005).

35. Marnia Lazreg, *Torture and the Twilight of Empire: From Algiers to Baghdad* (Princeton, NJ: Princeton University Press, 2008), p. 121.

36. Ibid., p. 253.

37. Allen Feldman, *Formations of Violence: The Narrative of the Body and Political Terror in Northern Ireland* (Chicago: University of Chicago Press, 1991), p. 5.

38. Brian Meeks has argued that the current crisis in the Caribbean is in part the result of the dissolution of hegemony. See Brian Meeks, *Narratives of Resistance* (Kingston, Jamaica: University of West Indies Press, 2000). David Scott has consistently argued this position about Bandung. See in particular David Scott, *Refashioning Futures: Criticism after Postcoloniality* (Princeton, NJ: Princeton University Press, 1999).

39. A section of this discussion of Jamaica has been published in various places. See in particular Anthony Bogues, "Power, Violence and the Jamaican 'Shotta Don'" *Report on the Americas*, special issue, *NACLA* 39, no. 6 (May–June 2006).

40. Achille Mbembe, *On the Postcolony* (Berkeley: University of California Press, 2001), p. 25.

41. The term "bare life" has become popular in contemporary Western political philosophy. It connotes a life that is limited to biological reproduction and that is distinguishable from the end of the politics, which is about human capacity and the structuring of common life. For slaves in Atlantic societies, very often not even bare life was permitted. For a discussion of bare life, see Andrew Norris, "Giorgio Agamben and the Politics of the Living Dead," in *Politics, Metaphysics and Death*, ed. Andrew Norris (Durham, NC: Duke University Press, 2005).

42. W. E. B. DuBois, *Black Reconstruction* (New York: Atheneum, 1962), p. 9.

43. See Diana Paton, *No Bond but the Law: Punishment, Race and Gender in Jamaican State Formation, 1780–1870* (Durham, NC: Duke University Press, 2004).

44. Horace Russell, "The Emergence of the Christian Black: The Making of a Stereotype," *Jamaica Journal* 16, no. 1 (1983): pp. 51–58.

45. Michel Foucault, *Power*, Essential Works of Foucault 1954–1984, vol. 3, ed. James D. Faubion, trans. Robert Hurley et al. (New York: New Press, 2000), p. 341.

46. This process is described in many texts, but see Philip Curtin, *Two Jamaicas: The Role of Ideas in a Tropical Colony, 1830–1865* (New York: Atheneum, 1970).

47. Cited in *Neither Led nor Driven*, p. 53.

48. Of course this reinterpretation belongs to two kinds of Afro-Jamaican religious practices, Rastafari and Native Baptist.

49. See of course Barry Chevannes's important study on Rastafari, Barry Chevannes, *Rastafari: Roots and Ideology* (Kingston, Jamaica: University of West Indies Press, 1995).

50. See Diane J. Austin-Broos, *Jamaica Genesis: Religion and the Politics of Moral Orders* (Kingston, Jamaica: Ian Randle Press, 1997).

51. Cited in Anthony Bogues, *Black Heretics, Black Prophets: Radical Political Intellectuals* (New York: Routledge, 2003), p. 191.

52. The figure of Ivan is based upon the Jamaican folklore character Rhyging.

53. Frantz Fanon, *The Wretched of the Earth* (New York: Grove Press, 1963), p. 94.

54. George Beckford, "Introduction" to Erna Brodber, *Standing Tall: Affirmations of the Jamaican Male* (Kingston, Jamaica: Sir Arthur Lewis Institute of Social and Economic Research, 2003), p. 29.

55. Terry Lacy, *Violence and Politics in Jamaica, 1960–1970* (Manchester: Manchester University Press, 1977), p. 28.

56. Ibid., p. 32.

57. Ibid., p. 33.

58. The definition of the relationship between clientage and political power is Carl Stone's. Cited in David Scott, "Rationalities of the Jamaican Modern," *Small Axe,* no. 14 (September 2003): p. 1.

59. Carl Schmitt, *The Concept of the Political* (Chicago: The University of Chicago Press, 1996), p. 26.

60. Ibid., p. 27.

61. The interviews on which this lecture is based were done in 1999 in an urban community that we will call Cascade Gardens. This community is an inner-city community that has had an extensive history of political violence and warfare. I want to thank the entire 1999 graduate class in Caribbean politics at the University of the West Indies for agreeing to participate in this project. Many of the interviews were conducted by them. Also thanks to Judith Wedderburn,

Veraldo Barnett, and Sherine Mackenzie, who worked with the project and made it possible. In particular I want to thank most profoundly the members of this community who spoke openly and shared many aspects of their lives with me. From them I have learned much that cannot be repaid.

62. Interview in Cascade Gardens, 1999. This can be translated roughly as, "anybody who is caught has to die. You will not allow your enemy to live." All the voices of those interviewed will be in Jamaican nation–language, and, when appropriate, I will translate.

63. Interview in Cascade Gardens, 1999. This is translated as "From you are informed by the sound of a stone hitting your fence, you know that you are asked to be up all night by some of the youths who are your friends. So you go and stay with them on the corner."

64. Ibid.

65. Lorna Goodison, "*Jamaica 1980*," in *Selected Poems* (Ann Arbor: University of Michigan Press, 1992), p. 38.

66. Hannah Arendt, *On Violence* (New York: Harcourt, Brace, and Company, 1969), p. 4.

67. See Michel Foucault, "Subject and Power," in Michel Foucault, *Power* (New York: New Press, 2000), pp. 326–48.

68. Achille Mbembe, "Necropolitics," *Public Culture* 15, no. 1 (2003): p. 11.

69. Interview in Cascade Gardens.

70. Rex Nettleford, *Inward Stretch, Outward Reach: A Voice from the Caribbean* (London: Macmillan Caribbean, 1993), pp. 80–90.

71. The closest it came to this hegemony was perhaps in the period between 1972 and 1977, during the regime of Michael Manley and the PNP government.

72. There are two types of area leaders in many communities. One type is deeply connected to the two-party political system, while the other is a semi-independent figure. It is the latter that I am concerned with. While I was proofreading this manuscript, the U.S. government requested the extradition of one of Jamaica's dons, Christopher Coke. After stalling for many months the Jamaican government agreed to this request. The move to execute the warrant for his arrest created (up to the time of this note) four days of violence in various parts of the island. The civilian death toll at this point (May 27, 2010) stands at seventy-three. In a profound sense Jamaican politics is today at a watershed moment as the "shotta don" becomes embedded within segments of the political and social system of the island.

73. See Diana Paton, *No Bond but the Law* (Durham, NC: Duke University Press, 2004). Paton observes that in nineteenth-century Jamaica, the existence of alternative justice systems depended upon the headman.

74. F. G. Cassidy and R. B. Le Page, in their classic *Dictionary of Jamaican English* (Kingston, Jamaica: University of West Indies Press, 2002), give us an important description of the duppy. The duppy is a ghost with a specific set of meanings in the Afro-Jamaican worldview. Cassidy and Page write of "The spirit of the dead, believed to be capable of returning to aid or more often to harm living beings" (p. 164). In my experience in rural Jamaica, people believe that duppies are ghosts who refuse to die and who are always around. It is felt that they have a life of their own and exist in passages between this world and another one. I think it is of some importance that the word is used by these urban young men in describing acts that result in the deaths of others.

75. Interview in Cascade Gardens, 1999.

76. Cited in Obika Gray, *Demanded but Empowered: The Social Power of the Urban Poor in Jamaica* (Kingston, Jamaica: University of West Indies Press, 2004), p. 244.

77. For a discussion of this and two case studies, particularly one in the community of August Town, see Horace Levy, "Peace in August Town" (unpublished paper).

78. Judith Butler, *Precarious Life* (London: Verso, 2004), p. 38.

Chapter 4: The End of History or the Invention of Existence

1. Walter Benjamin, "Theses on the Philosophy of History," in *Illuminations: Essays and Reflections of Walter Benjamin*, ed. Hannah Arendt (New York: Schocken Books, 1968), p. 257.

2. For a discussion of slavery, see in particular Aristotle, *Politics*, ed. Steven Everson (Cambridge: Cambridge University Press, 1988), Book 1.

3. Ibid.

4. For a discussion of the centrality of 1492 and Columbus's voyages, see Sylvia Wynter, "1492: A New World View," in *Race, Discourse, and the Origins of the Americas*, ed. Vera Hyatt and Rex Nettleford (Washington, D.C.: Smithsonian Institution, 1995), pp. 5–57.

5. *Free-dom*. I am separating the word to linguistically mark the relationship between domination and imperial freedom that I have been working with throughout this lecture series.

6. Alex Callinicos, *Theories and Narratives: Reflections on the Philosophy of History* (Cambridge: Polity Press, 1995), p. 165.

7. Walter Benjamin, "Theses on the Philosophy of History," in *Illuminations* (see note 1), p. 262.

8. Sylvia Wynter, "Jonkonnu in Jamaica: Towards the Interpretation of the Folk Dance as a Cultural Process" *Jamaica Journal* 4, no. 2 (June 1970): 35.

9. Georg Hegel, *Lectures on the Philosophy of World History* (Cambridge: Cambridge University Press, 1975), p. 19.

10. Ibid., p. 53.

11. From www.whitehouse.gov/stateofunion/2003/index.html.

12. For a discussion of this, see Jean-Luc Nancy, *The Creation of the World, or, Globalization* (Albany: State University of New York Press, 2007), chapter 1.

13. Stuart Hall, "The West and the Rest: Discourse and Power," in *Formations of Modernity*, ed. Stuart Hall and Bram Gieben (Cambridge: Polity Press, 1992), pp. 275–332.

14. Ibid.

15. Hannah Arendt, *The Promise of Politics* (New York: Schocken Books, 2005), p. 40.

16. Clifford Geertz, *Local Knowledge* (Boston: Basic Books, 1983), chapter 8.

17. Of course the term *critical theory* is usually associated with the Frankfurt Institute for Social Research and was initially derived from the work of the various members of the Frankfurt School: Adorno, Fromm, Horkheimer, Marcuse, and Benjamin. Intellectually, the term has its roots in a Kantian critique and in Marx's critique of ideology. My argument is that the framing of the many questions asked by various members of this school of thought was shaped by the emergence of Fascism as a catastrophic event.

18. Cited in Richard Tuck, *Hobbes: A Very Short Introduction* (Oxford: Oxford University Press, 2002), p. 29.

19. Thomas Hobbes, *The Leviathan* (New York: Prometheus Books, 1988). The entire fourteenth chapter of this seminal text is taken up with the explication, in different ways, of the establishment of the social contract, seen in political theory as the originary formation of political society. Of course the masculine and racial nature of this contract has come under severe and, to my mind, justifiable critique. See in particular Carole Pateman and Charles Mills, *Contract and Domination* (Cambridge: Polity Press, 2007).

20. See Bryan Edwards, *The History, Civil and Commercial of the British West Indies*, vol. 2 (Philadelphia: 1806), p. 32.

21. Paul Ricoeur, *History and Truth* (Evanston, IL: Northwestern University Press, 1965), p. 34.

22. When thinking about the question of the human today, one is of course confronted with the remarkable developments in the fields of genetics and neuroscience. However, as critical as these new developments are, I do not believe they constitute a basis for discussing a definitive post-human stage for humankind. What is most human in us is not that we are biologically determined but

that we are socially and culturally shaped. Therefore as a species we are capable of change and adaptation. For an attempt to think about how the post-human need not be anti-human, see N. Katherine Hayles, *How We Became Post Human* (Chicago: University of Chicago Press, 1999).

23. John Edgar Wideman, *Fanon* (New York: Houghton Mifflin Company, 2008), p. 222.

24. Stuart Hall, "The Afterlife of Frantz Fanon: Why Fanon? Why Now? Why *Black Skin, White Masks?*" in *The Fact of Blackness: Frantz Fanon and Visual Representation*, ed. Alan Read (Seattle: Bay Press, 1996), p. 14.

25. Lewis Gordon, *Fanon and the Crisis of European Man* (New York: Routledge, 1995), p. 86.

26. Charles H. Long, *Significations: Signs, Symbols and Images in the Interpretation of Religion* (Aurora, IL: Demes Group Publishing, 1995), p. 212. I want to thank my colleague Corey Walker for introducing me to the work of Charles Long.

27. Ato Sekyi-Otu, *Fanon's Dialectic of Experience* (Cambridge, MA: Harvard University Press, 1996), p. 4.

28. Fanon, *Black Skin, White Masks*, p. 217.

29. Ibid.

30. Ibid., p. 220.

31. Ibid.

32. Ibid.

33. Ibid., pp. 220–21.

34. Ibid.

35. For the classic discussion in English about the revolution, see C. L. R. James, *The Black Jacobins* (London: Allison and Busby, 1980).

36. This can be discerned from the many historical accounts of ex-slave life in post-emancipation Caribbean society. For example, see Frank McGlynn and Seymour Drescher, eds., *The Meaning of Freedom* (Pittsburgh: University of Pittsburgh Press, 1992); Frederick Cooper, Thomas Holt, and Rebecca Scott, eds., *Beyond Slavery* (Chapel Hill: University of North Carolina Press, 2000).

37. See Kojeve's discussion of Hegel's work in Alexandre Kojeve, *Introduction to the Reading of Hegel* (Ithaca, NY: Cornell University Press, 1980), especially chapter 1.

38. Carolyn Fick, *The Making of Haiti: The Saint Domingue Revolution from Below* (Knoxville: University of Tennessee Press, 1990), p. 179.

39. For a discussion of this, see Anthony Bogues, "The slave work so do we, what's the difference," in *Caribbean Thought and the Radical Imagination* (Princeton, NJ: Markus Wiener, 2010). For a full discussion of the Haitian Revolution and its meanings for freedom in the modern world, see Anthony Bogues, *Singing Songs of Freedom: Freedom and Black Radical Intellectual Tradition* (forthcoming).

40. The evidence is sufficient to understand the Haitian Revolution as a dual revolution. The first revolution abolished slavery and culminated in the 1801 Constitution promulgated by Toussaint L'Ouverture. The second revolution was the one for political independence, marked by the Haitian Declaration of Independence of 1804.

41. Cited in Fanon, *Black Skin, White Masks*, p. 223.

42. Aimé Césaire, *Notebook of a Return to My Native Land*, trans. Mireille Rosello and Annie Pritchard (Newcastle Upon Tyne, UK: Bloodaxe Books, 1995), p. 117.

43. Fanon, *Black Skin, White Masks*, p. 225.

44. For a discussion of dread history, see Anthony Bogues, *Black Heretics and Black Prophets: Radical Political Intellectuals* (New York: Routledge, 2003).

45. Fanon, *Black Skin, White Masks*, p. 222.

46. Ibid., p. 229.

47. Ibid.

48. Ibid., p. 231.

49. Ibid., p. 232.

50. In a set of conversations with me, John Edgar Wideman has insisted that we call the "new humanism" a radical humanism. He may be right, not only because we need to rethink what the human means in humanism, but because we need to do so from a radical perspective, one that opens up new categories of thought.

51. For a discussion, see Michel Foucault, *The Order of Things: An Archaeology of the Human Sciences* (New York: Vintage, 1994), chapter 10.

52. For a fuller discussion of this point, see Anthony Bogues, "And What about the Human? Radical Anti-Colonial Thought and Critical Thinking," in *Who Can Act for the Human?* ed. Taieb Belghazi, Mohammed Ezroura, and Ronald Judy (Rabat, Morocco: Mohammed V University, Publications of the Faculty of Letters and Human Sciences, 2009), pp. 51–63.

53. Fanon, *Black Skin, White Masks*, p. 232.

54. Frantz Fanon, *The Wretched of the Earth* (New York: Grove Press, 1963), p. 316.

55. David Macy, *Critical Theory* (London: Penguin, 2000), p. 74.

56. For a selection of the writings of this school, see Andrew Arato and Eike Gebhardt, eds., *The Essential Frankfurt School* (London: Continuum, 2007).

SELECTED BIBLIOGRAPHY

Agamben, Giorgio. *Homo Sacer: Sovereign Power and Bare Life.*
Stanford, CA: Stanford University Press, 1998.
———. *State of Exception.* Chicago: University of Chicago Press, 2005.
Althusser, Louis. *On Ideology.* London: Verso, 2008.
Arendt, Hannah. *Eichmann in Jerusalem.* In *The Portable Hannah
Arendt,* edited by Peter Baehr, pp. 313–75. New York: Penguin,
2000.
———. *The Human Condition.* Chicago: University of Chicago Press,
1998.
———. "The Image of Hell." In Hannah Arendt, *Essays in
Understanding,* edited by Jerome Kohn, p. 197. New York: Schocken
Books, 1994.
———. *On Revolution.* London: Penguin, 1965.
———. *On Violence.* New York: Harcourt, Brace, and Company, 1969.
Austin-Broos, Diane J. *Jamaica Genesis: Religion and the Politics of
Moral Orders.* Kingston, Jamaica: Ian Randle Press, 1997.
Bacevich, Andrew J., ed. *The Imperial Tense: Prospects and Problems of
American Empire.* Chicago: Ivan R. Dee, 2003.
Bauman, Zygmunt. *Consuming Life.* Cambridge: Polity Press, 2007.
Beckford, George. "Introduction" to Erna Brodber, *Standing Tall:
Affirmations of the Jamaican Male,* pp. 382–89. In *The George
Beckford Papers,* selected and introduced by Kari Levitt. Kingston,
Jamaica: Canoe Press, University of the West Indies, 2000.
Benjamin, Walter. "Theses on the Philosophy of History." In
Illuminations: Essays and Reflections of Walter Benjamin, edited by
Hannah Arendt, pp. 253–64. New York: Schocken Books, 1968.

Bercovitch, Sacvan. *The American Jeremiad*. Madison: University of Wisconsin Press, 1978.

Bogues, Anthony. "And What about the Human? Radical Anti-Colonial Thought and Critical Thinking." In *Who Can Act for the Human?* edited by Taieb Belghanzi, Mohammed Ezroura, and Ronald Judy, pp. 51–63. Rabat, Morocco: Mohammed V University, Publications of the Faculty of Letters and Human Sciences, 2009.

———. *Black Heretics, Black Prophets: Radical Political Intellectuals*. New York: Routledge, 2003.

Bourdieu, Pierre. *Language and Symbolic Power*. Cambridge, MA: Harvard University Press, 1995.

Burchell, Graham. "Peculiar Interests: Civil Society and Governing 'The System of Natural Liberty.'" In *The Foucault Effect: Studies in Governmentality*, edited by Graham Burchell, Colin Gordon, and Peter Miller, pp. 119–50. Chicago: University of Chicago Press, 1999.

Burnett, Christina, and Burke Marshall, eds. *Foreign in a Domestic Sense*. Durham, NC: Duke University Press, 2001.

Bush, George. "America's Responsibility, America's Mission." In Andrew Bacevich, *The Imperial Tense*, pp. 5–9. Chicago: Ivan R. Dee, 2003.

Callinicos, Alex. *Theories and Narratives: Reflections on the Philosophy of History*. Cambridge: Polity Press, 1995.

Caruth, Cathy. *Unclaimed Experience: Trauma, Narrative, and History*. Baltimore: Johns Hopkins University Press, 1996.

Cassidy, F. G., and R. B. Le Page. *Dictionary of Jamaican English*. Kingston, Jamaica: University of West Indies Press, 2002.

Césaire, Aimé. *Notebook of a Return to My Native Land*, translated by Mireille Rosello and Annie Pritchard. Newcastle Upon Tyne, UK: Bloodaxe Books, 1995.

Chevannes, Barry. *Rastafari: Roots and Ideology*. Kingston, Jamaica: University of West Indies Press, 1995.

Conklin, Alice. *A Mission to Civilize: The Republican Idea of Empire in France and West Africa, 1895–1930*. Stanford, CA: Stanford University Press, 1997.

Cooper, Robert. "The New Liberal Imperialism." In *The Observer*, April 7, 2002.

Curtin, Phillip. *Two Jamaicas: The Role of Ideas in a Tropical Colony, 1830–1865*. New York: Atheneum, 1970.

Dayan, Colin. *The Story of Cruel and Unusual*. Cambridge, MA: MIT Press, 2007.

Dubois, W. E. B. *Black Reconstruction, 1860–1880*. New York: Atheneum, 1962.

———. "Marxism and the Negro Problem." In *W. E. B. Du Bois: A Reader*, edited by David Levering Lewis, p. 543. New York: Henry Holt and Company, 1995.

———. *The Souls of Black Folk*. New York: Dodd, Mead and Company, 1961.

Dunn, John, ed. *Democracy: The Unfinished Journey, 508 BC–AD 1993*. Oxford: Oxford University Press, 1993.

Edwards, Bryan. *The History, Civil and Commercial of the British West Indies*. Vol. 2. Philadelphia: 1806.

Fanon, Frantz. *Black Skin, White Masks*. New York: Grove Press, 1967.

———. *The Wretched of the Earth*. New York: Grove Press, 1963.

Feldman, Allen. *Formations of Violence: The Narrative of the Body and Political Terror in Northern Ireland*. Chicago: University of Chicago Press, 1991.

Ferguson, Niall. *Colossus: The Price of American Empire*. New York: Penguin Press, 2006.

Fick, Carolyn. *The Making of Haiti: The Saint Domingue Revolution from Below*. Knoxville: University of Tennessee Press, 1990.

Fischer, David Hackett. *Liberty and Freedom: A Visual History of America's Founding Ideas*. Oxford: Oxford University Press, 2005.

Foner, Eric. *The Story of American Freedom*. New York: Norton, 1998.

Foucault, Michel. *Discipline and Punish: The Birth of the Prison*. New York: Vintage, 1995.

———. *"Society Must Be Defended": Lectures at the Collège de France, 1975–1976*. New York: Picador, 2003.

———. "The Subject and Power." In Michel Foucault, *Power*, edited by James D. Faubion, pp. 326–48. New York: New Press, 2000.

Freud, Sigmund. *Beyond the Pleasure Principle*. New York: Norton, 1989.

Gooding-Williams, Robert. *Look, A Negro: Philosophical Essays on Race, Culture and Politics*. New York: Routledge, 2006.

Goodison, Lorna. *Selected Poems*. Ann Arbor: University of Michigan Press, 1992.

Gordon, Lewis. *Fanon and the Crisis of European Man*. New York: Routledge, 1995.

Goveia, Elsa. *The West Indian Slave Laws of the 18th Century*. Barbados: Caribbean Universities Press, 1970.

Gray, John. *Two Faces of Liberalism*. New York: New Press, 2000.

Greenberg, Karen J., and Joshua Dratel. *The Torture Papers: The Road to Abu Ghraib*. Cambridge: Cambridge University Press, 2005.

Guillén, Nicolás. *Man-Making Words: Selected Poems of Nicolás Guillén*, translated by Roberto Marquez and David McMurray. Amherst: University of Massachusetts Press, 1972.

Hall, Catherine. *Civilizing Subjects*. Chicago: University of Chicago Press, 2002.

Hall, Stuart. "The Afterlife of Frantz Fanon: Why Fanon? Why Now? Why *Black Skin, White Masks*?" In *The Fact of Blackness: Frantz Fanon and Visual Representation*, edited by Alan Read, pp. 14–28. Seattle: Bay Press, 1996.

———, ed. *Representation: Cultural Representations and Signifying Practices*. London: Sage Publications, 2003.

———. "The Toad in the Garden: Thatcherism among the Theorists." In *Marxism and the Interpretation of Culture*, edited by Cary Nelson and Lawrence Grossberg, pp. 35–74. Urbana: University of Illinois Press, 1988.

———. "The West and the Rest: Discourse and Power." In *Formations of Modernity*, edited by Stuart Hall and Bram Gieben, pp. 275–332. Cambridge: Polity Press, 1992.

Hardt, Michael, and Antonio Negri. *Empire*. Cambridge, MA: Harvard University Press, 2000.

Hartman, Saidiya. *Scenes of Subjection*. New York: Oxford University Press, 1997.

Hatzfeld, Jean. *Machete Season: The Killers in Rwanda Speak*. New York: Picador, 2003.

Hegel, Georg. *Lectures on the Philosophy of World History*. Cambridge: Cambridge University Press, 1975.

Hobbes, Thomas. *The Leviathan*. New York: Prometheus Books, 1988.

Hobson, J. A. *Imperialism*. New York: Gordon Press, 1975.

Holt, Thomas. *The Problem of Freedom*. Kingston, Jamaica: Ian Randle Press, 1992.

How Race Is Lived in America. New York: Times Books, 2001.

James, C. L. R. *The Black Jacobins*. New York: Vintage, 1989.

————. *The Future in the Present*. London: Allison and Busby, 1977.

Kaplan, Amy. *The Anarchy of Empire in the Making of U.S. Culture*. Cambridge, MA: Harvard University Press, 2002.

LaCapra, Dominick. *Writing History, Writing Trauma*. Baltimore: Johns Hopkins University Press, 2001.

Laclau, Ernesto. *Emancipation(s)*. London: Verso, 1996.

Lazreg, Marnia. *Torture and the Twilight of Empire: From Algiers to Baghdad*. Princeton, NJ: Princeton University Press, 2008.

Leach, William. *Land of Desire: Merchants, Power, and the Rise of a New American Culture*. New York: Vintage Books, 1994.

Levi, Primo. *The Voice of Memory: Interviews, 1961–1987*, edited by Marco Belpoliti and Robert Gordon. New York: New Press, 2001.

Levinson, Sanford, ed. *Torture: A Collection*. Oxford: Oxford University Press, 2004.

Leys, Ruth. *Trauma: A Genealogy*. Chicago: University of Chicago Press, 2000.

Lieven, Dominic. *Empire: The Russian Empire and Its Rivals*. London: John Murray, 2000.

Long, Charles H. *Significations: Signs, Symbols and Images in the Interpretation of Religion*. Aurora, IL: Demes Group Publishing, 1995.

Loury, Glenn. "Ghettoes, Prisons and Racial Stigma." The Tanner Lectures, April 4, 2007, copy provided by author.

Luban, David. "Liberalism, Torture, and the Ticking Bomb." In *The Torture Debate in America*, edited by Karen J. Greenberg, pp. 35–83. Cambridge: Cambridge University Press, 2006.

Lukes, Steven, ed. *Power*. New York: New York University Press, 1986.

Macy, David. *Critical Theory*. London: Penguin, 2000.

Magdoff, Harry. *Imperialism without Colonies*. New York: Monthly Review Press, 2003.

Manet, Pierre. *An Intellectual History of Liberalism*, translated by Rebecca Balinski. Princeton, NJ: Princeton University Press, 1995.

Mbembe, Achille. "Necropolitics." *Public Culture* 15, no. 1 (2003): pp. 11–40.

———. *On the Postcolony*. Berkeley: University of California Press, 2001.

———. *On Private Indirect Government*. Dakar, Senegal: CODESRIA, 2000.

Meeks, Brian. *Narratives of Resistance*. (Kingston, Jamaica: University of West Indies Press, 2000).

Mills, Charles. *The Racial Contract*. Ithaca, NY: Cornell University Press, 1997.

Morrison, Toni. "The Site of Memory." In *Inventing the Truth: The Art and Craft of Memoir*, edited by William Zinsser, pp. 183–200. Boston: Mariner Books, 1998.

Moses, A. Dirk, and Dan Stone, eds. *Colonialism and Genocide*. London: Routledge, 2007.

Nancy, Jean-Luc. *The Creation of the World, Or, Globalization*. Albany: State University of New York Press, 2007.

Norris, Andrew, ed. *Politics, Metaphysics and Death*. Durham, NC: Duke University Press, 2005.

Pagden, Anthony. *Peoples and Empires*. New York: Modern Library, 2001.

Paton, Diana. *No Bond but the Law*. Durham, NC: Duke University Press, 2004.

Pease, Donald. "9/11: When Was 'American Studies After the New Americanists'?" *boundary* 2 (Fall 2006).

———. "Tocqueville's Democratic Thing; or, Aristocracy in America." In *Materializing Democracy: Toward a Revitalized Cultural Politics*, edited by Russ Castronovo and Dana Nelson, pp. 22–52. Durham, NC: Duke University Press, 2002.

Rancière, Jacques. *Disagreement*. Minneapolis: University of Minnesota Press, 1999.

———. *On the Shores of Politics*. London: Verso, 1995.

Ricoeur, Paul. *History and Truth*. Evanston, IL: Northwestern University Press, 1965.

Robinson, Cedric. *Black Marxism*. London: Zed Press, 1987.

Russell, Horace. "The Emergence of the Christian Black: The Making of a Stereotype." *Jamaica Journal* 16, no. 1 (1983): pp. 51–58.

Scarry, Elaine. *The Body in Pain*. Oxford: Oxford University Press, 1985.

Schmitt, Carl. *The Concept of the Political*. Chicago: University of Chicago Press, 1996.

Scott, David. *Refashioning Futures: Criticism after Postcoloniality*. Princeton, NJ: Princeton University Press, 1999.

Sekyi-Otu, Ato. *Fanon's Dialectic of Experience*. Cambridge, MA: Harvard University Press, 1996.

Shklar, Judith. "Positive Liberty, Negative Liberty in the United States." In Judith Shklar, *Redeeming American Political Thought*, edited by Stanley Hoffman and Dennis Thompson, chapter 8. Chicago: University of Chicago Press, 1998.

———. "Putting Cruelty First." *Daedalus* 111, no. 3 (Summer 1982): pp. 17–27.

Singh, Nikhil Pal. *Black Is a Country*. Cambridge, MA: Harvard University Press, 2004.

Smallwood, Stephanie. *Saltwater Slavery: A Middle Passage from Africa to American Diaspora*. Cambridge, MA: Harvard University Press, 2007.

Smith, Rogers. *Civic Ideals*. New Haven, CT: Yale University Press, 1997.

Tocqueville, Alexis de. *Democracy in America*. Vol. 1. New York: Vintage Books, 1990.

———. *Democracy in America*. Edited by J. P. Mayer. Translated by George Lawrence. 2 vols. New York: Perennial, 2000.

Wideman, John Edgar. *Fanon*. New York: Houghton Mifflin Company, 2008.

Williams, Raymond. *Keywords: A Vocabulary of Culture and Society*. Oxford: Oxford University Press, 1983.

———. *The Long Revolution*. Peterborough, Ontario: Broadview Press, 2001.

Williams, William Appleman. *Empire as a Way of Life*. Oxford: Oxford University Press, 1980.

Winant, Howard. *The New Politics of Race*. Minneapolis: University of Minnesota Press, 2004.

Wolin, Sheldon. *Politics and Vision*. Princeton, NJ: Princeton University Press, 2004.

————. *Tocqueville between Two Worlds: The Making of a Political and Theoretical Life*. New Haven, CT: Yale University Press, 2007.

Wynter, Sylvia. "1492: A New World View." In *Race, Discourse, and the Origins of the Americas*, edited by Vera Hyatt and Rex Nettleford, pp. 5–57. Washington, D.C.: Smithsonian Institution, 1997.

————. "On How We Mistook the Map for the Territory and Re-imprisoned Ourselves in Our Unbearable Wrongness of Being, of *Désêtre*: Black Studies Toward the Human Project." In *Not Only the Master's Tools: African-American Studies in Theory and Practice*, edited by Lewis R. Gordon and Jane Anna Gordon, 107–69. Boulder, CO: Paradigm Press, 2006.

abolition, 7, 59–60, 67, 81–82, 113
Abu Ghraib, 32–34, 134n30
Adorno, Theodor, 29–30, 138n17
Afghanistan, 77
Agamben, Giorgio, 29, 31–32
Algeria, 49, 78–79, 125n37
Althusser, Louis, 2, 23–24
American Black Power movement, 85
American Colonization Society
    (ACS), 52–53, 131n45
American exceptionalism, 27
American power: as deployment of
    democracy/freedom, 11–12,
    14–16; as imperial power, 9, 26;
    nation building and, 124n12;
    stages of consolidation of, 16; as
    structure of feeling, 25
American Revolution, 57–58, 102
American Samoa, 34
Arendt, Hannah: "banality of evil"
    principle, 71–72; on colonial
    power, 21; on "dark times"
    historical exceptionalism, 101–2;
    on genocide, 69, 71; on political
    power, 16, 120; on revolution,
    57–58; on violence as means-end
    instrument, 90–91; on violence vs.
    power, 73–74, 101; on Western
    political silence, 107
Aristotle, 6, 97, 100

Armenian genocide, 69
Augustine, Saint, Bishop of Hippo, 6
Austin-Broos, Diane, 83

Badiou, Alan, 102
Baker, Ella, 63
"banality of evil" principle, 71
"bare life," 82, 134n41
Barlow, Joel, 15
Bataille, Georges, 93
Battle of Algiers, The, 78
Bauman, Zygmunt, 25
Beaumont, Gustave de, 130n37
Beckford, George, 85
Benjamin, Walter, 99, 103, 119,
    138n17
Bercovitch, Sacvan, 22
Beveridge, Albert, 15
bio-politics, 4–5, 7, 17–18, 35,
    123n5
bios-politics, 17–18
black internationalism, 43–44
black nationalist movement, 92–93
Black Reconstruction, 53–54, 64–65,
    67, 131n46. See also DuBois,
    W. E. B.
body: domination of the body in
    slavery, 31, 39–40, 82; genocidal
    death and, 72–74; post-humanism
    and, 138n22; racial domination

body (*continued*):
    and, 39–40, 46; sovereign power
    and, 31, 70–71; torture of
    excluded bodies, 77, 133n30;
    traumatic saturation of, 44;
    violence and, 90
Bounti Killa, 94
Bourdieu, Pierre, 35
Boyd, Julian, 13–14
British Empire, 26
Burchell, Graham, 36
Burke, Edmund, 5, 13
Bush, George W., 4–5, 21–22, 24–25,
    76–78, 105
Butler, Judith, 97

Callinicos, Alex, 102–3
Caruth, Cathy, 41–42
Casas, Bartolomé de las, 108
Castoriadis, Cornelius, 63
Castro, Fidel, 85
Césaire, Aimé, 21, 116
Cherokee Nation v. State of Georgia
    (1831), 34
Churchill, Winston, 12
Cicero, 11, 35
citizenship: American liberalism and,
    27; in Greek democracy, 99–100;
    imperial citizens, 29; racial
    exclusion and, 31–34, 85; in the
    Roman empire, 14
civilization, 20, 21
civil rights movement, 45, 63, 85
Clay, Henry, 52–53, 131n45
Cliff, Jimmy, 84
colonialism: as arena of historical
    questioning, 107–8; coercive fear
    as necessity, 109; colonial power,
    20–21, 81–83, 125n37; critical
    theory and, 119; genocide and,
    68–69, 75; historical treatment of,

78–79; locus of colonial power,
    26. *See also* colonial modernity
colonial modernity: coloniality-
    modernity relationship, 78,
    127n71; effect on contemporary
    life, 107, 109, 121; emergence of
    liberalism and, 21; historical and
    social trauma and, 100; liberty
    and, 37; representation and, 62
Columbus, Christopher, 6, 100–101
common sense, 4, 36
Commune in Paris, 102
Communism, 85–86
Conklin, Alice, 20
conscience, 18–19
constitutional representativeness, 67
consumption, 19–20, 25
Cooper, Robert, 22–23
Crashaw, William, 28
critical theory, 8, 119–20, 138n17
cruel and unusual punishment,
    32–34, 78
Cuban Revolution, 85–86
Curtin, Phillip, 83

Dayan, Colin, 30, 32, 78
death: as definitive of humanity, 97;
    genocidal death, 72–74; historical
    dialogue with the dead, 116–17;
    as performance of power, 7; as
    self-fashioning spectacle, 93–94,
    101, 137n74; social death,
    30–31, 82
democracy: as empty signifier, 61–63,
    67, 99–100; equality as principle
    of, 38–39, 46–48, 79–80;
    historical wrongs relationship
    with, 64–65; liberty as principle
    of, 48; limits of imperial democ-
    racy, 79–80; as process vs.
    experience, 7, 46–47, 62–65;

slavery as problem for, 7, 49–50, 59–60, 130n37; as universal truth, 11–12, 14–15, 21–22, 59; *zoon politikon* concept and, 6

Democracy in America, 47–53, 64–65, 67, 130n37. *See also* Tocqueville, Alexis de

Demosthenes, 61

Derrida, Jacques, 105–6

Descartes, René, 109

desire: in American imperial power, 12; bio-political power and, 17–18; consumption and, 19–20, 25; invoked by "strong words," 15; pastoral power and, 18–19; as soft power, 25

Dewey, John, 61

diaspora, 43–44

domestic dependent nations, 34, 99

domination: liberty as, 36–37; political subjectivity, 16–18; racial domination as historical moment, 12; self-regulating *free-dom* and, 101–2, 105, 120, 137n5; slavery as social death, 82

double structure of liberalism, 27–29, 32, 37

Douglas, Mary, 74

Douglass, Frederick, 39–40, 131n45

dread history, 116–17

Dred Scott case, 30, 78

DuBois, W. E. B.: on abolition democracy, 7, 59–60, 67; as anti-imperialist writer, 2–3; on black invisibility, 44; *Black Reconstruction*, 53–54, 64–65, 67, 103, 131n46; on detached witnessing, 46; on domination in slavery, 82; on emancipation, 58–59; sites of exception and, 99

Dunn, John, 61

Dussell, Enrique, 8

economy: American Revolution and, 57–58; consumption as desire, 19–20, 25; ethic of the market, 3–4; slavery as economic force, 55–56, 59–60; wage labor in Marxism, 114–15

Edwards, Bryan, 109

Eichmann, Adolf, 71

empire: defined, 10–11; as civilizing mission, 11; as logic and structure of rule, 10; as single unique power, 10–11, 124n9; totalizing capacity of, 66–67

"empire of liberty" concept: American Century project and, 5; constitutional representativeness and, 67; death as horizon in, 97; "empire of democracy" in Tocqueville, 48–49; imperial liberalism and, 23; Jeffersonian concept of, 13–14; reformulation of, 98–99; self-regulation and, 67

Enlightenment, 12

epistemological location, 102

equality: democracy as representation of, 38–39, 46–47, 61–63, 79–80; racial inequality, 27–28; in Tocqueville, 27, 48–50

ethic of the market, 3–4

Ethiopianism, 43–44

executions, 77

failed states, 33–34, 77–78, 128n75. *See also* nation-states

Fanon, Frantz: on colonial power, 21; critical views on, 110–12; formulation of history by, 116–17; on invention, 117–18,

Fanon, Frantz (*continued*):
121; on Marxist social revolution,
115–16; radical humanism of,
117–19; on slavery, 40; on
traumatic saturation of the black
body, 44–45; on violence, 73–74,
84–85
Fascism, 12, 21, 107
Feldman, Allen, 80
Fick, Carolyn, 114
Fisher, Katherine, 19
flogging, 82, 86
Foucault, Michel: on bio-politics, 7,
17, 35, 123n5; on Enlightenment
as historical moment, 12; on
liberal power, 21; on pastoral
power, 18–19; on the political
body, 74; on political subjectivity,
16–17; on power as productive
force, 81; on punishment, 77; on
sovereign power, 31, 70–71; on
the sovereignty of the subject,
118; on the thematics of power, 75
Frankfurt School, 119, 138n17
Freedman Humanities Lecture Series,
1–3, 5–6
freedom: as civil rights ambition,
63–64; consumption and, 19–20,
25; ethic of the market and, 4;
Fanon ontology of freedom,
117–18; imperial freedom, 5–6;
as negation of life, 101; perspective of the unfree and, 8; as
political *free-dom*, 66–67, 101–2,
105, 120, 137n5; slave freedom,
31, 56, 67, 113–15; as universal
truth, 11–12, 14–15, 21–22; wage
labor and, 114–15
French Empire: French abolition
movement, 113–14; historical
treatment of, 78–79; *mission*

civilisatrice in French colonialism,
20; territory as fundamental to,
26; Tocqueville support for, 49,
125n37; torture as component of,
79–80
French Revolution, 102
Freud, Sigmund, 41–42, 110
Fromm, Erich, 138n17
Fukuyama, Francis, 105

Gama, Vasco da, 6
Garvey, Marcus, 43–44, 92–93
Geertz, Clifford, 107
genetics, 138n22
Geneva conventions, 77
genocide: overview, 68–75, 90;
colonialism and, 68–69, 75; as
performance of power, 7; as
racial cleansing, 70–71; social
conditions for, 69–70; sovereign
power and, 70–71; as spectacle
of purification, 71–72. *See also*
violence
German Empire, 26, 69–70
Godelier, Maurice, 99–100
Gooding-Williams, Robert, 44
Goodison, Lorna, 89
Gordon, Lewis, 110
Goveia, Elsa, 30, 100
Gramsci, Antonio, 4, 36
Gray, John, 22
Greek democracy, 61, 99–100,
132n67
Guam, 34
Guantánamo Bay naval base, 32–34
Guevara, Che, 85
Guillén, Nicolás, 30
Guyana, 80–81

Haile Selassie, 85
Haiti, 49, 55, 140n40

Haitian Revolution, 49, 53, 55, 113–15, 140n40
Hakluyt, Richard, 28
Hall, Stuart, 2, 23–24, 62, 106, 110
Harder They Come, The, 84
Hardt, Michael, 10
Hartman, Saidiya, 39
Hartz, Louis, 27
Hegel, Georg Wilhelm Friedrich, 104–7, 110, 112–14
hegemony: imperial freedom compared with, 11–12; as mode of domination, 17; obscurity of alternatives by, 26; racial domination and, 45; violence and, 134n38
Heidegger, Martin, 109
Henzell, Perry, 84
Herero genocide, 69–70
historically catastrophic events, 38–39, 40, 58–59, 102–3, 107. *See also* trauma
history: advent of "man" in, 109; Arendt "dark times" historical exceptionalism, 101–2; colonialism and, 78–79; Enlightenment and, 12; fascism and, 12; Hegelian "end of history," 104–10; historical telos as closure, 105–6; historical trauma, 41–44; historical vs. structural trauma, 43; historical wrongs and democracy, 64–65; liberalism and, 12; production of freedom from, 116–17; racial domination and, 12; states of exception and, 98–99. *See also* historically catastrophic events
Hobbes, Thomas, 18, 107–8, 138n19
Hobson, J. A., 26

Holocaust, 69, 74
Horkheimer, Max, 138n17
Hughes, Langston, 37
humanity: abrogation of rights and, 109; anti-colonial tradition and, 8; death as definitive of humanity, 97; democratic subjectivity and, 6; *homo oeconomicus*, 25; humanness as constitutive of freedom, 121; human perfectibility, 20; logic of affliction and, 83; natural liberty and, 36; normative *anthropos* perspective, 109; post-humanism, 138n22; racial classification, 7; radical humanism, 118, 140n50; slavery and, 40, 42, 51
imperial citizens, 29
imperial freedom: defined, 5–6; *free-dom* domination relationship, 101–2, 105, 120, 137n5; hegemony compared with, 11–12; regeneration/creativity in, 15; representation/discourse and, 5–6; self-regulation and, 10, 12; slavery and, 58–59
inclusion/exclusion: construction of democracy and, 7, 47–48, 55, 65; in Greek democracy, 99–100; "political kingdom" as civil rights ambition, 63–64; racial exclusion, 31–34, 85; torture and, 77, 134n30
instituting events, 100–101
International Monetary Fund (IMF), 1–2
invention, 117–18, 121
Iraq War, 4–5. *See also* Bush, George W.; September 11, 2001; terror

Jamaica: decolonization effects in,
1–2; duppy figure, 93, 137n74;
ethnographic research project on,
88, 135n61; Jamaican colonial
rule, 82–83; Jamaican peace
movement, 94–96; political
violence, 80–81, 86–90; Rude
Bwoy figure, 84–86, 94; Shotta
Don figure, 92–97, 101, 136n72
James, C. L. R., 3, 53, 55, 62
Jefferson, Thomas, 5, 13–14, 52
Judy, Roland, 4

Kafka, Franz, 72
Kant, Immanuel, 12, 138n17
Kaplan, Roger, 14
King, Martin Luther, Jr., 63
Kohl, Helmut, 3–4
Kojeve, Alexandre, 113–14

Lacan, Jacques, 25, 110
LaCapra, Dominick, 40, 43
Laclau, Ernesto, 2, 61
Lacy, Terry, 85–86
language: American liberty as
speech-act, 34–36; colonial power
and, 21; desire in "strong words,"
15; genocide and, 71–72; Logos
as ideology, 23–24; the West as
generative epistemological
concept, 106
Lazreg, Marnia, 79
Leach, William, 19
Lemkin, Raphel, 68
Levellers, 62
Levi, Primo, 72
Levinas, Emmanuel, 107
Leys, Ruth, 41
liberalism: dilemma of violence and,
16–17, 20–21, 133n30; genealogy
of American liberalism, 28; as

historical moment, 12; imperial
liberalism, 22–23; liberalism of
rights, 27–28; sites of exception
for, 31–34; socialism and, 27
liberty: as domination, 36–37;
Jeffersonian concept of, 5, 13–14;
natural liberty, 13, 36–37; as
normalized polity, 36; self-
government and, 13, 61; as
self-regulated political freedom,
66–67; as structure of feeling,
24–25; Tocqueville concept of,
34, 48
Lieven, Dominic, 10
livity, 120
Locke, John, 13, 18, 27, 30
logic of affliction, 83
Long, Charles, 111
Loury, Glenn, 44–45
Luban, David, 76
lynching, 133n30
Lyotard, Jean-François, 106

Madison, James, 52–53
Manent, Pierre, 10–11
Marcuse, Herbert, 138n17
Marley, Bob, 92–93, 93–94
Marx, Karl, 112
Marxism: class violence in Jamaica
and, 86–87; DuBois influence by,
60; Frankfurt School critical
theory, 119, 138n17; social
revolution in, 115–16; wage
labor as slavery in, 114–15
Massop, Claude, 94–95
Massu, Jacques, 79
May 1968 events, 102
Mbembe, Achille, 20, 91
Mead, Fogg, 19
Meeks, Brian, 134n38
Mexican War, 15

Mill, John Stuart, 21
Mills, Charles, 34
modernity, 78, 100–101, 121, 127n71. *See also* colonial modernity
Morrison, Toni, 42

Nambia, 69
Nancy, Jean-Luc, 106
nation building, 124n12
nation-states: black nationalist movement, 92–93; consolidation of freedom in, 104; domestic dependent nations, 34, 99; failed states, 33–34, 77–78, 128n75; legitimacy of power in, 17; nation building, 124n12; sovereignty relationship with, 18
Native Americans, 15–16, 34, 50, 99
Nazism, 107
necropolitics, 16–17
Negri, Antonio, 10
neoliberalism, 4, 22–23
Nettleford, Rex, 92
neuroscience, 138n22
Nietzsche, Friedrich, 80, 104–5
Nye, Joseph, 25

Paine, Thomas, 15
Parsons, Talcott, 74–75
pastoral power, 18–19
Paton, Diana, 82
Patterson, Orlando, 30–31, 81–82
Paul, the Apostle, Saint, 24
Pease, Donald, 28–29, 47
Pericles, 61
Peterson, Merrill, 5
Pinckney, Thomas, 13
Pocock, J. P., 27
politics of the radical imagination, 120

Pontecorvo, Gillo, 78
Portuguese Revolution, 102
power: death/violence as performance of, 7; as opposite of violence, 73–74, 101; pastoral power, 18–19; politics of being and, 120; self-regulating *free-dom* and, 101–2, 105; soft power, 25; thematics of power, 75. *See also* American power
Price, Richard, 13
prisons, 78
Puerto Rico, 34
punishment: cruel and unusual punishment, 32–34, 78; public executions, 77; school flogging in Jamaica, 86; slave beatings, 32, 39, 82

race/racism: classification of human beings and, 6–7; debasement argument and, 52; racial contract, 34; racial exclusion from the body politic, 31–34, 69–70, 85; Tocqueville on racial superiority, 50
racial domination: black incarceration rates, 44–45, 47; contemporary practice of, 121; as historical moment, 12; racism as repetition of the wound of slavery, 44; slavery as ultimate degradation, 53; slavery as violence, 39–40; as state of exception, 40
racial inequality, 27–28
radical humanism, 118, 140n50
Rancière, Jacques, 7, 56, 61, 65, 129n5
Randolph, John, 52–53
Rastafari, 83–86, 88, 92, 94–96, 120

Reagan, Ronald, 3–4
religion: Afro-Christian subjectivity, 82–83; Bush administration theo-political philosophy, 105; emancipation and, 56–57, 58–59; Hegelian "end of history" and, 104–5; pastoral power, 18–19; Puritan Idealism as universal democracy, 59; Rastafari, 83–86, 88, 92, 94–96, 120; virgin land doctrine and, 28
republic (form of government), 10
res nullius doctrine, 28
revolution: epistemological location and, 102; imperial freedom and, 57–59; slavery and, 49, 53, 55. See also *particular revolutions*
Ricoeur, Paul, 109
rights: abrogation of rights, 107–9; coercive domination vs. self-regulation and, 45; freedom as civil rights ambition, 63–64; liberalism of rights, 27–28
Roman empire, 14
Rude Bwoy, 84–86, 94
Rumsfeld, Donald, 76–77
Russell, Horace, 82
Rwandan genocide, 68–69, 71, 74

Scarry, Elaine, 74, 76
Schmitt, Carl, 87–88
security: empire of liberty and, 97; Jamaican violence and, 86–87; liberalism and, 17, 23; liberty synonymous with, 36; post-9/11 Homeland Security State, 28–29; sovereignty and, 18
Sekyi-Otu, Ato, 112
self-government, 3–4, 13, 26, 61–63
self-regulation: bio-politics and, 17–18; consumption and, 19–20;

hegemony compared with, 11–12; imperial freedom and, 10, 12; liberty constructed from, 66–67; as political *free-dom*, 101–2, 105, 120
September 11, 2001, 28–29, 76–78
Sepúlveda, Juan Ginés de, 108
Shklar, Judith, 27–28, 76
Singh, Nikhil, 53
sites of exception, 31–34, 99
slavery: abolition as civilizing mission, 21; abolition of Jamaican slavery, 81–82; abrogation of rights and, 108–9; American Revolution and, 57–58; black abolitionism, 113; civil vs. social death and, 30–31; classification of human beings and, 6–7; colonial power and, 81–83; debasement argument and, 52; democracy incompatibility with, 7, 49–50, 59–60, 130n37; in Greek democracy, 99–100, 132n67; master-slave dialectic, 112–14; ontological legacy of, 29–30, 112–14; pastoral power and, 19; prison system as legacy of, 78; racial slavery as "property in the person," 55, 100; recolonization movement, 52–53, 131n45; role in American imperialism, 16; as site of exception, 99; slave freedom, 31, 56, 67, 113–15; as social death, 82, 134n41; sovereign power and, 31; as traumatic event, 42–44; violence as fundamental to, 39–40
Smallwood, Stephanie, 42–43
Smith, Roger, 27
soft power, 25
Solon, 100

Sontag, Susan, 70
sovereignty: colonial sovereignty, 20; individualization/totalization procedures in, 18–19; political obligation and, 16–18; self-government fundamental to, 26; sovereign power, 31, 70–71, 107–8; violence fundamental to, 70–71, 91
Soviet Union, 102
Spanish Civil War, 102
speech-acts, 34–36
states of emergency, 99
states of exception: overview, 29–30; ahistorical character of, 98–99; domestic dependent nations, 34; racial domination as, 40; sites of exception and, 31–34, 99
Stephens, Thaddeus, 59
St. Lucia, 80–81
"strong words" (Williams), 15
Student Nonviolent Coordinating Committee (SNCC), 63
subjectivity: Afro-Christian subjectivity, 82–83; agency as a material practice, 80; colonial subjectivity, 21; Fanon ontology of freedom, 117–18; political obligation and, 16–18; reciprocal recognition in slavery, 112; slavery as social death, 82
sufferers, 83

Taney, Roger, 30, 78
territory, 10, 18, 26, 34
terror, 70–72, 76–78
Thatcher, Margaret, 3–4
Thirteenth Amendment (U. S. Constitution), 78
Thompson, Aston "Buckie," 94–95
Thucydides, 61

Tocqueville, Alexis de: on American liberty, 34; on colonial power, 125n37; *Democracy in America*, 47–53, 64–65, 67, 130n37; "empire of democracy" in, 48–49; equality vs. liberty in, 47–48; on French colonialism, 49, 125n37; Hartz influence by, 27; on innate equality, 27; on race and slavery, 49–50, 130n37
torture: overview, 90; in the Algerian War of Independence, 79; contemporary practice of, 120; destruction of the self in, 74; interrogation and, 76–77, 134n30; liberalism and, 23; sites of exception and, 32–34; as spectacle, 133n30; violence and, 76–80
Tosh, Peter, 85, 96
Toussaint L'Ouverture, 140n40
trauma: civil rights movement treatment of, 63–64; historical vs. structural trauma, 43; politics of the wound, 40; racial slavery as, 42–44; social legacy of, 38–39; trauma studies, 41; witnessing of, 44. *See also* historically catastrophic events; violence
Trinidad, 80–81
Trotha, Lothar von, 70
Turnipseed v. State (1844), 32

Universal Negro Improvement Association, 43–44
urban poor, the, 80

violence: overview, 90–92; colonial power and, 20, 125n37; death as spectacle and, 93–94; Jamaican political violence, 86–90;

violence (*continued*):
Jamaican Rude Bwoy violence, 84–86, 94; neoliberalism and, 23; as opposite of power, 73–74, 101; as performance of power, 7; political vs. intimate violence, 90; sovereignty relationship with, 70–71, 91; torture and, 76–80. *See also* genocide; trauma
Virgin Islands, 34
virgin land doctrine, 28

Waldron, Jeremy, 78
Washington, Busrod, 52–53
Washington, George, 52–53
ways of life: American liberty as model, 12, 14, 16; consumption and, 25; critical view of, 120; imperial power and, 21–22; practice of democracy and, 6, 61; practice of freedom and, 8; self-regulation and, 17
Weber, Max, 74–75

Webster, Daniel, 52–53
Wideman, John Edgar, 110, 140n50
Williams, Eric, 55
Williams, Raymond, 15, 20, 24
Williams, William Appleman, 16
Winant, Howard, 45
witnessing, 44, 46, 77, 133n30
Wolin, Sheldon, 28–29, 48–49
World Bank, 1–2
World Trade Center attack. *See* September 11, 2001
wounds: historical dialogue with, 116–17; politics of the wound, 40, 129n5; racism as repetition of the wound of slavery, 44; revolution and, 57–58
wrongs, 40, 64, 129n5
Wynter, Sylvia, 25, 36, 103

X, Malcolm, 92–93

zoon politikon, 6